Era of Transition

The **Institute of Southeast Asian Studies (ISEAS)** was established as an autonomous organisation in 1968. It is a regional research centre for scholars and other specialists concerned with modern Southeast Asia, particularly the many-faceted issues and challenges of stability and security, economic development, and political and social change.

The Institute's research programmes are Regional Economic Studies (RES, including ASEAN and APEC), Regional Strategic and Political Studies (RSPS), and Regional Social and Cultural Studies (RSCS).

ISEAS Publications, an established academic press, has issued more than 1,000 books and journals. It is the largest scholarly publisher of research about Southeast Asia from within the region. ISEAS Publications works with many other academic and trade publishers and distributors to disseminate important research and analyses from and about Southeast Asia to the rest of the world.

Era of Transition
Malaysia after Mahathir

Ooi Kee Beng

LSEAS

Institute of Southeast Asian Studies
Singapore

First published in Singapore in 2006 by
Institute of Southeast Asian Studies
30 Heng Mui Keng Terrace
Pasir Panjang
Singapore 119614

Internet e-mail: publish@iseas.edu.sg
World Wide Web: http://bookshop.iseas.edu.sg

This book is published under the Malaysia Study Programme
funded by Professor Saw Swee-Hock.

Design by Sara Ooi

*The responsibility for facts and opinions in this publication
rests exclusively with the author and his interpretations
do not necessarily reflect the views or the policy of the
Institute or its supporters.*

ISEAS Library Cataloguing-in-Publication Data

Ooi, Kee Beng, 1955-
    Era of Transition: Malaysia after Mahathir.
    1. Malaysia—Politics and government—1963-
    2. United Malays National Organisation.
    3. Islam and state—Malaysia.
    4. Regionalism—Southeast Asia.
    5. ASEAN.
    6. Southeast Asia—Foreign relations.
    I. Title
DS597.2 O62   2006

ISBN 981-230-379-0

Printed in Singapore by Seng Lee Press Pte Ltd

*Lovingly dedicated
to my loving wife Laotse
and my beautiful babies
Sara, Cian and Aoife*

CONTENTS

On Islam and Nation Building

On Regionalism and Globalisation

One Country,
Two Leaders, Three Q's

Q: "What will happen to Malaysia without Mahathir?"

That was the question repeatedly asked by Malaysians and others after Dr. Mahathir Mohamed announced his intention to relinquish his post as the Prime Minister of Malaysia in July 2002. The timing was intriguing in itself, and many perceived his retirement to be coming at the height of his success.

We have had more than two years now to find satisfactory answers, and they reveal a rather interesting mix of responses – some pessimistic, some optimistic and the rest merely uttering a fate-accepting sigh of "*Que sera sera*".

To foreigners who had invested heavily in Malaysia, the departure of Mahathir was worrying because he was perceived as *the* architect of Malaysia's phenomenal economic growth over the last two decades, who steered the ship of state through two major economic crises – the first in 1985-86 and the second bigger one in mid-1997. Indeed, he has been viewed as being responsible for the opening up of the economy to foreign investors and for launching Malaysia into the K-Economy orbit. His astute political skill and judgment and, particularly, his sense of timing, had enabled him to survive two major political crises within his own political party, UMNO, namely, the 1987 UMNO crisis and the 1998 Anwar Ibrahim-related crisis.

With such a tremendous and unparalleled record of achievement, it was not surprising at all that pessimists were doubtful whether his successor, Abdullah Badawi, would be able to equal, let alone improve on, Mahathir's record. Indeed, some chose to consider Abdullah weak, ineffective, non-charismatic, to be without a clear vision of Malaysia's future, and incapable of mobilizing the population to greater heights, both in the economic and political spheres.

Interestingly, some quarters within UMNO itself quietly shared this pessimistic view. These were members who feared that their political and economic future was threatened by Mahathir's departure. As usual, the realism of the optimists has served as a useful antidote to the 'chaos theory' of the pessimists.

According to the latter, we must locate the issue of Mahathir's resignation in a broader context, in fact within the giant canvas of the whole of the socio-economic history and politics of Malaysia.

It was also often emphasized that we could not afford to be overly sentimental about Mahathir. Even if we were to clone Mahathir, like scientists have done with the sheep Polly and Dolly, the cloned version, with differences in upbringing and socialization, would in politically relevant ways not be like the original Mahathir at all. For all we know, such the clone might turn out to be more suitable as a member of *Parti Islam*!

In the longitudinal historic sense, Mahathir definitely occupies a special position in Malaysia's post-colonial history. However, he is far from being the only one to fit that revered position in Malaysia's history. There are a number of such personalities, each contributing to the laying of the country's foundation as well as the shaping of Malaysia into what it is today.

There was Dato' Onn Jaafar, the man who invented UMNO. There was Tunku Abdul Rahman, Malaysia's first prime minister, who invented the first coalition party in Malaysia, the Alliance, and who negotiated for Independence, together with Tan Cheng Lock and Sambanthan. Tunku Abdul Rahman also negotiated for the formation of Malaysia with Lee Kuan Yew of Singapore, Tun Mustapha and Donald Stephens of Sabah and Abdul Rahman Yaakub and Temenggong Jugah of Sarawak.

There was also Abdul Razak Hussein, who created the National Front with Tan Siew Sin and V. Manickavasagam. Together they rebuilt Malaysia after the racial riot of 1969. Razak was the architect of the pro-Malay affirmative action policy, that is, the New Economic Policy of 1991-1990. There was also Dr Ismail bin Abdul Rahman, the tough loyalist who guaranteed the country's belief in the rule of law.

Then came Mahathir. He became Prime Minister in 1981. He built Malaysia into what it is now, partly basing himself on the solid economic and political foundations laid by his predecessors. Of course, he had his own ideas about what Malaysia should become and he implemented his ideas in his own style, sometimes abrasively and sometimes not, but his passion for power, success and glory never escaped anyone.

Many of us in Malaysia would have liked Mahathir to always have played along with the common idealism of "the means justifying the end." But sometimes, Mahathir preferred the reverse, and the end would be used to justify the means. For that Mahathir has been both revered and resented, by his countrymen and others.

One thing is certain though. During his period in power, Mahathir laid new economic, political and socio-cultural foundations that he thought would best prepare Malaysia for a stable future.

The man's belief in this calling is the legacy that he has left Malaysia and Malaysians. Indeed, it is this legacy that Abdullah Badawi must build upon, and alter where necessary. When Abdullah took over, the pressing question was the following:

Q2: "Is Abdullah Badawi a leader who is capable enough to manage Mahathir's legacy properly?"

Answers to this are aplenty. In fact, many articles and books, both in Malay and English, have appeared over the last couple of years to provide insights on the matter, and on issues that stem from it.

However, it is way too easy for us to forget the fact that it has only been two years since Abdullah became prime minister. Many think it quite unfair to judge his performance based only on such a short period of time. It would be even more grossly unfair to compare the achievements and failures of Abdullah two-year regime to those of Mahathir's 22-year rule.

This has been done, nevertheless, especially within Abdullah's own political party, UMNO. This is not surprising. After all, if we adopt Abdullah's role-model concept of "towering Malay," Mahathir was one who fits that label very well. If we apply Abdullah's slogan *"cemerlang, gemilang, terbilang"* (excellence, glory, distinction), Mahathir, too, seems to be the one person in Malaysia to have achieved this.

Now, if Mahathir has been a "towering Malay" who sought *"cemerlang, gemilang, terbilang"*, we need nevertheless to ask the question "what was the price of his success?" How is Abdullah to deal with Mahathir's complex legacy of success and failure? How does Abdullah find his own space and niche, and one easily and immediately differentiated from the dense and overpowering shadow of Mahathir?

We may have to wait for some years to really provide detailed, in-depth and satisfactory answers to these questions. The question of the moment remains the following.

Q3: How has Abdullah fared in the last 24 months?

The present volume, entitled *Era of Transition: Malaysia after Mahathir*, which is a collection of Dr. Ooi Kee Beng's previously published commentaries, provides the best informed analysis to date not only on Abdullah's first 24 months as a prime minister but also Malaysia's 24 months without Mahathir. The commentaries are succinct and lucid, spiced with significant historical anecdotes, conceptually suggestive, and cover issues ranging from domestic to regional matters, as well as international and personal ones about both the leaders.

The main thread that holds the commentaries together throughout this volume is that the legacy that Mahathir leaves behind is as much about the struggle to limit collateral damage as it is about enjoying his achievements. Dr. Ooi Kee Beng, however, argues that we must at the same time be conscious of the fact that the achievement-damage complex predates Mahathir, and even Malaysia's founding, and that colonial conceptions are still highly relevant to the analysis of the new nation's political thought. In some cases, the latter continues to exert decisive influence. He therefore offers a fresh perspective for us to reflect not only on the immediate two years of the post-Mahathir era, and Abdullah Badawi's performance in the last 24 months, but also about the uniqueness of the Malaysian experience. Of course, not everyone will agree with all his opinions. But this in no way lessens the value and significance of his comments, and we should be grateful that he is willing to share them with us.

Professor Shamsul A.B.
Director
ATMA & IKON
Universiti Kebangsaan Malaysia

ACKNOWLEDGEMENTS

The person whom I wish to thank most is the Director of ISEAS, Ambassador K. Kesavapany, whose faith in my ability to opine meaningfully on Malaysian events even as they happen provided the main impetus for these endeavours. Being what he himself calls a "generalist", he encouraged researchers such as myself to test the waters beyond the comfortable shores of their disciplines and training, and to venture into the exciting world of the commentator.

Without encouragement from Singapore's major newspaper, The *Straits Times*, for fresh and topical commentaries for its Review pages, most of the pieces found in this collection would not have been written at all. I therefore owe its editorial staff a heartfelt shout of thanks. Gratitude is also owed to *Asia Times Online* and *Project Syndicate*.

I wrote these commentaries while coordinator for ISEAS' Malaysia Study Programme, which is funded by Professor Saw Swee-Hock. I happily take this opportunity to express my deepest appreciation for his support and generosity. Another Very Important Person I would like to thank – very belatedly no doubt – is Mr Anthony Gomez, my English language teacher from St Xavier's Institution in Penang. It was he who through surprising pedagogical innovations taught me early in life that it is we who make use of language, and not *vice versa*.

ABOUT THE AUTHOR

Dr OOI KEE BENG was born in Penang, receiving his basic education at La Salle School and St Xavier's Institution.

He is presently a Fellow at Singapore's Institute of Southeast Asian Studies (ISEAS), where he coordinates its Malaysia Study Programme. His fields of interest include modern language philosophy, Chinese philosophy, nation building with a special focus on Malaysia, political economics and the philosophy of science. He has degrees in Public Administration and Chinese Language Studies, as well as a doctorate in Sinology, all from Stockholm University, Sweden, where he also lectured in Chinese Philosophy, Chinese History and General Knowledge of China between 1995 and 2004.

He has published in *Tonan Ajia Kenkyu* (Southeast Asian Studies), *3L* – Journal of Language Teaching, Linguistics and Literature, *SARI – Journal of the Malay World and Civilization*, *Melayu – Jurnal Antarabangsa Dunia Melayu*, *Orientaliska studier*, *Regional Outlook*, and *Southeast Asian Affairs* on subjects ranging from modern language philosophy and Chinese philosophy to Malaysian politics and the Chinese Diaspora. His books include *The State and its Changdao: Sufficient Discursive Commonality in Nation Renewal, with Malaysia as Case Study; Chinese Studies of the Malay World: A Comparative Approach* in collaboration with Ding Choo Ming, as well as translations of Chinese military classics into Swedish, such as *Wei Liao Zis krigskonst*, *Wu Zis krigskonst* and *Sunzis krigskonst*.

He also writes regular commentaries for Singapore's *Straits Times* on Malaysian politics and socio-economics.

He is presently working on a biography titled *The Reluctant Politician: Tun Dr Ismail and His Time*, the anthology *The State of Vision 2020: Conceptual Challenges to Malaysia's Progress*, as well as the book *Staggered Decolonization & Steadied Construction: Malaysian Nation Building and the Current Epistemic Revolution*.

INTRODUCTION

No Success without Collateral Damage

If there is any common point being made throughout this collection of commentaries on Malaysian political life after Mahathir Mohamed's retirement in October 2003, it is that all formulas for success are plagued by what I wish to call "collateral damage".

As with undertows in rapid currents, the very fact that policies and their rationale must simplify the world in order to be practicable creates spirals that whirl outward, sideward, downward and *backward* at a pace decided by the dynamic of the central thrust, as well as by the resistance to it.

As with collateral damage in war, so it is with policy-making. Sometimes, unfavourable results are taken into account beforehand as part of the price that has to be paid. Oftentimes, side effects – even powerful ones – continue unnoticed for long periods. Left to themselves, they can easily develop to a point where they actually threaten to reverse the major flow itself.

Politics is opportunistic and pragmatic by nature. Subsequently, political discourses are essentially prescriptive structures meant to direct thought and action along paths illumined by chosen parameters. In the case of Malaysia, the foundation stones of political discourse were as much "Malay Special Rights", "non-Malay citizenship rights" and the infamous "Internal Security Act" as they were "transparency", "parliamentary monarchy" and "the rule of law".

From these principles and contingencies grew a system of consociational politics that soon evolved into the hegemony of the strongest component party, the United Malays National Organisation (UMNO). A "model" – imperfect yet not ineffectual – slowly came into being. From 1970 onwards, the dual motors of political change in Malaysia were the dynamics of Islamization and the affirmative action policy called the New Economic Policy (NEP).

Mahathir had throughout this period until his retirement in October 2003 been a permanent fixture in the corridors of power. His 1970 book – *The Malay Dilemma* – was at that time the most articulate, if not always accurate, expression of feelings of injustice felt by large segments of the Malay population. Although sacked in 1969 from UMNO for his bald criticism of the first Prime Minister, Tunku Abdul Rahman, he soon attained a position of power when the next Prime Minister, Tun Abdul Razak Hussein, brought him in from the cold in 1974 and made him Minister of Education. He went on to be elected UMNO vice president in 1975. After Razak passed away from leukaemia in January 1976, Mahathir managed to ascend to the position of Deputy Prime Minister under the next national leader, Tun Hussein Onn. In 1978, he became Minister for Trade and Industry.

On 16 July 1981, he rose to the top of the pyramid as Malaysia's fourth prime minister. For 22 years after that, he stayed in power, surviving a long series of challenges along the way, even as he pushed the country towards becoming an economic powerhouse that could not be ignored.

However, his strong and sustained influence over Malaysian nation building has meant that collateral damage from his policies has been widespread, significant – and lasting. The legacy he leaves behind is therefore as much about the struggle to limit detrimental side effects as it is about enjoying his achievements. To be fair, far from the full blame for collateral damages should be placed on him, just as it would be erroneous to ascribe the whole credit for the country's success to his leadership. The achievement–damage complex predates Mahathir, and even Malaysia's founding logic, along with stubborn colonial conceptions, are still highly relevant for the analysis of the new nation's political discourses. The section on regionalism and globalisation illustrates this point.

Nevertheless, the onus of office for Mahathir's successor, Abdullah Badawi, stems to a significant extent from the character and the actions of the former, as do the stature of the premiership itself and the centralised structure of Malaysia's politics.

The commentaries in this selection are specifically about the first two years and more of Abdullah's premiership. Unfortunately, that period in office saw the death on Thursday morning, 20 October 2005, of his wife, Endon Mahmood. How this will affect his style of politics is for the future to decide.

In a wider perspective, these opinion pieces should also be understood as humble attempts made partly to elucidate a definite stage in Malaysia's nation building and partly to analyse the wider phenomenon that is Abdullah's fate – that of succeeding a Great Leader in a new nation.

Interestingly, this fate has been common to many contemporary leaders throughout the world. In that sense, various points raised in this volume comprise relevance beyond the specific time and the special place that inspired them. They are meant to testify to the uniqueness of the

Malaysian experience and to the generality of human issues at one and the same time.

All the chapters were previously published, but for this occasion, some minor changes have been made.

Ooi Kee Beng

On Umno and Malaysia

1

Umno smoothly alters the Malay agenda

DEMOCRACY IN Malaysia functions at three levels - within the United Malays National Organisation (Umno), the leading party of the ruling National Front; among members of the National Front itself; and in the general elections.

Of these three, Umno party elections are the most free, the campaigns most fearless, and the results most significant to national politics.

More than that, both the talk and the walk at the party's general assemblies are largely indicative of the mood of the majority Malays, and of their take on the state of the nation.

What Umno decides anchors national policies, and what Umno talks about, the country as a whole cannot ignore.

The president of Umno, who is invariably also the prime minister, must, therefore, choose his words well in addressing party members, because he cannot help but speak to all his countrymen at the same time. This, Prime Minister Abdullah Ahmad Badawi did in a gallant manner at the party's 55th general assembly.

The congress was held in an atmosphere of euphoria, buoyed by unsurpassed government success in the March general election and by what many consider a closure on the painful Anwar Ibrahim episode, following his release from prison earlier this month.

Malay unity, so fragile in 1999, is stronger than ever under the banner of Umno.

The Parti Islam SeMalaysia (PAS) has been taught a lesson that it will find hard to forget; and Parti Keadilan Rakyat, led by Datuk Seri Anwar's wife, is now but a frail force.

When the previous Umno president, Tun Dr Mahathir Mohamad, gave his maiden speech at the Umno general assembly in 1981, nothing was said about Islamic reforms. However, the recruitment of Datuk Seri Anwar the following year was done largely to satisfy demands from more religious factions.

Datuk Seri Abdullah's 100-minute speech, on the other hand, starts off with an elaborate account of his newly coined term, Islam Hadhari (Civil Islam). This comes before such vital issues as foreign policy and even 'the Malay agenda', indicating the importance the regime now must attach to the question of Islam.

However, the message throughout the speech - that the Malays must seek knowledge, capacity and competitiveness - is strongly tied to the promulgation of Islam Hadhari, which appears more and more to be a commendable and viable discursive innovation for altering the world view and self-identity of the Malay majority.

There is much to feel optimistic about in Datuk Seri Abdullah's speech, especially his morally informed call for a mental revolution that must involve a knowledge-seeking Islam, acceptance of the global lingua franca, and adequate attention to quality in the advancement of the Malays as a group.

Especially encouraging is his confession that affirmative action had perpetuated prejudices that it was meant to eradicate, such as that of bumiputeras 'lacking competitiveness and durability'.

'If we are honest with ourselves, we will accept the fact that those who get something too easily have no real, no intrinsic, strength. There can be no self-worth for those who obtain positions, business opportunities and scholarships without real effort and qualification,' he said.

Calls for gender equality within Umno Wanita, for party mass democracy by Tengku Razaleigh Hamzah, and for permanently closed doors to party 'traitors' by Umno Youth chief Hishamuddin Hussein, added colour to a congress that analysts had looked forward to.

The biggest surprises came in the poll results, when as many as three Cabinet ministers - Information Minister Paduka Abdul Kadir Sheikh Fadzir, who had held his party position since 1984, Home Affairs Minister Azmi Khalid and Higher Education Minister Shafie Salleh - lost their seats on the 25-member Supreme Council, along with seven of the 17 other incumbents seeking re-election.

All three female candidates, however, were voted in.

The most dramatic results were those for the three posts of vice-president. Agriculture and Agro-based Industry Minister Muhyiddin Yassin was tipped to remain first vice-president, an outcome preferred by Datuk Seri Abdullah, who had been talking about investing in growth in the agricultural sector. In the event, he received only 1,234 votes, behind Federal Territories Minister Mohamed Isa Abdul Samad (1,507) and Malacca Chief Minister Ali Rustam (1,329).

Personality appears to have been a deciding factor and, given the fact that the Abdullah administration is new, voting for a succession was probably not the intention of most delegates.

While Datuk Hishamuddin remains Umno Youth leader, being returned uncontested to the post, this son of Malaysia's third premier Hussein Onn and grandson of Umno founder Onn Jaafar will be assisted by his new No. 2, Mr Khairy Jamaluddin, son-in-law of Datuk Seri Abdullah, who also won uncontested.

These thoroughbreds are joined by Tun Dr Mahathir's youngest son, Datuk Mukhriz Mahathir, in the executive council. Datuk Mukhriz surprisingly received the most votes among the 20 exco members, only two of whom were incumbents.

Puteri Umno, founded only in 2001 for women members who are under 36, opted on the other hand for continuity with 12 incumbents being returned to their seats, most of them in the top 10 positions.

Umno's young seem to have the requirements for climbing the party ladder and are now, furthermore, well placed to play decisive roles in Malaysia's political future. If Malay self-confidence and willingness to accept change are vital to the interracial harmony in Malaysia, as Umno's leaders seem to think, then things look good.

We must hope that the party as a whole takes full responsibility for ruling what is a multiracial country badly challenged by global forces, as much as its new leader apparently intends to.

First published in Commentary/Analysis, *Straits Times*, 27 September 2004. Reproduced with the kind permission of Singapore Press Holdings.

2

Fighting the money game
in Umno elections

CAN THERE be democracy without money, surprises and contestation of ideas?

If a dilemma is a situation where none of the thinkable outcomes is welcome, then Malaysian Prime Minister Abdullah Badawi must have been experiencing one recently.

Had those whom he favoured been victorious in the Umno party elections last month, then there would have been talk about how party democracy was controlled by the party top; and had his favourites lost, some of whom obviously did, then there is immediate speculation about money politics instead.

Were votes bought at the party's 55th general assembly? Probably, possibly and almost certainly. However, there is little that Datuk Seri Abdullah or his deputy, Datuk Seri Najib

Abdul Razak, can do without sufficient evidence, and definition, of wrongdoing.

When clear guidelines as to what constitutes money politics are missing, then one must expect some candidates to push the limits until they get a smack on their hands. Abiding by intuitive rules when much is at stake has never been a human strong point.

Punishing delegates for allowing their votes to be bought would be a possible approach if not for the impossibility of ascertaining guilt. Furthermore, those whose votes are being paid for would be the best witnesses against corruption, which means that establishing the guilty party may be effective with some moral encouragement at the lower end. Being approached by a vote-buyer should more be perceived privately and publicly as an embarrassment and an insult that must be stopped.

When is one winning votes and when is one buying them? Buying votes has obviously become entrenched in Umno elections. No one denies that. Former premier Mahathir Mohamad himself shed public tears over it.

In recent months, 22 people were suspended for one term (three years) and warnings were issued to 11 others. In the run-up to the general assembly, the disciplinary committee received as many as 400 complaints.

Open campaigning about ideas and issues would be a way out, but that easily leads to conflicts and harsh words. That is its nature. Since that was minimised for fear of splitting the party, the question is, if the contest of divergent views is avoided for the sake of race unity, party uniformity, or whatever reason one can think of, then are candidates pushed to profile themselves through the cultivation of charisma and visibility? And if that does not seem to work, the temptation to buy or curry favour, which of course involves money, will be quite irresistible, and even indispensable, especially to outsider candidates.

What conclusion are we to draw from this? Is Umno lacking in democratic maturity, or must we admit that democracy is a money game?

Electoral structure has a definite impact on the preponderance of money politics. Indeed, we are dealing with the larger issue of how Umno, or any other party for that matter, is constructed. If a candidate can profile himself only through 'meeting the grassroots' - meaning the 2,520 delegates representing 190 divisions - then personal contacts, favours and understandings must quickly come into the picture.

Paradoxically, money politics - understood as the buying of singular votes - will be less effective and therefore less tempting the more money it costs, and the more voters there are to buy. If direct democracy as suggested by former finance minister Tengku Razaleigh Hamzah is imposed, where all 3.2 million Umno members have voting rights, then campaigning will have to be in the form of mass meetings, and the skills consequently needed will stretch beyond the arranging of tea parties or the pushing of fat envelopes under hotel doors.

Money politics, then, is directly connected to restrictions on idea contestation and to power centralisation, and is not a problem that is specifically Umno's. The election surprises to the supreme council immediately raised suspicions about money being used, although surprises are surely a common outcome in democratic processes.

What was, in fact, surprising was that the upsets surprised so strongly, and that improprieties were automatically suspected. This tells us something about what electoral predictability indicates instead, and about campaign rituals in general.

'Leadership by example' can only go a certain distance. Thereafter, Datuk Seri Abdullah, if his drive to fight corruption at all levels of society is not to appear quixotic, has no choice but to put on iron gloves to curb money politics, knowing as he well does that party men carrying a stigma of corruption cannot now or later command authority and respect. Having such politicians does not bode well for the party or the nation.

Self-respect includes respect for one's representatives, and is indispensable to the pride and confidence that Malaysians of all races must feel for the nation-building process to have succeeded.

First published in Commentary/Analysis, *Straits Times,* 1 October 2004. Reproduced with the kind permission of Singapore Press Holdings.

3

A year of ruling comfortably

DATUK SERI Abdullah Ahmad Badawi has now been the fifth prime minister of Malaysia for exactly a year.

While the claim that his period is but transitional - after Tun Dr Mahathir Mohamad, although before what or whom is never made clear - no longer makes sense, a general notion persists that his position is weak and his ambitions as prime minister are hampered by a lack of support within his party, the United Malays National Organisation (Umno).

The beating taken by some candidates who are generally considered his supporters at the recent party elections seemed to strengthen this suspicion. However, if that was the case, the exercising last week of the party president's prerogative of appointing 12 members to the Supreme Council and of filling other important positions must have regained him much ground.

One dubious explanation for his style of leadership is that he was a civil servant as a young man in the 1960s and 1970s.

One must remember at the same time, however, that he has been in political life ever since the time of the third prime minister, Tun Hussein Onn. His political acumen and experience cannot be doubted, and his patient and tolerant personality should not be mistaken for weakness.

If Tun Dr Mahathir's style was that of the impatient hare, Datuk Seri Abdullah's must be that of the focused tortoise. The tortoise has a more peaceful time than the hare, as we know, and a quick look at Datuk Seri Abdullah's first year in office tells us that he does keep his eye on the ball and allows things to take the time they need.

Datuk Seri Abdullah's style is clearly different from that of his predecessor. His problems are different, and his situation is different. Umno is more streamlined than ever, the Barisan Nasional is united to an enviable degree, the Islamist challenge has been effectively met, and ideas of the Reformasi have been partly co-opted.

The release of former deputy premier Anwar Ibrahim has also strengthened the Prime Minister's reputation as a fair man, and his decision to leave the judicial apparatus alone has been loudly applauded.

Where his international stature is concerned, the lucky fact that Malaysia is currently chairing both the Organisation of Islamic Conference (OIC) and the Non-Aligned Movement (NAM) has given Datuk Seri Abdullah a lot of free international coverage, providing him with the chance to offer Malaysia as a venue for an open international discourse on Islam.

At the beginning of the month, the international financial magazine The Emerging Markets voted him and his financial deputy Nor Mohamed Yakcop Asia's best finance ministers. This exposure has contributed much to his standing at home and abroad. Economically, therefore, there is little to complain about. Growth will almost certainly reach the projected 7 per cent, while the stock market continues on an upward trend. International recognition also includes Standard & Poor's upgrading of the political economy's currency ratings. The GDP deficit is down to 4.5 per cent from the average of 8 per cent over the last few years, with 3.8 per cent planned for next year. Most government-linked companies have also managed encouragingly well.

It is still a little early to pronounce a verdict on how Datuk Seri Abdullah's war on graft is faring. But Malaysia's fall in world ranking on the Transparency Corruption Perception Index recently made public, to share a spot with Tunisia, shows a worrying ineffectuality in the Abdullah factor. However, it needs to be considered that graft is now so much a part of the Malaysian way of life that active administrative and public support cannot be counted on. This makes it all the more necessary for the government to institute uncompromising measures to end this acceptance of corruption.

The fact that the Anti-Corruption Agency is not totally independent, for example, does not help public perception of governmental inability to fight ingrained corruption. Aid from outside the system, or the country, should not be discounted as an effective option in this vitally important reform.

His refusal to grant a soccer gambling licence to businessman Vincent Tan's Ascot Sports on Oct 19, together with his shelving last December of what would have been the country's most expensive investment, the double-track railway project that had already been awarded to Malaysian mining corporation Gamuda, shows laudable moral sense on his part. Both licences were approved in principle during Tun Dr Mahathir's term in office, the former only four months before he stepped down.

The coining of Islam Hadhari to articulate the tradition of moderate Islamic practice at the very beginning of Datuk Seri Abdullah's term, and the use of the slogan

'Work with me' during the general election are his most memorable innovations. These still gain him political points, and Islam Hadhari's mildly formulated principles allow for negotiations as to how Islam is to work in a multicultural nation.

On the international front, Islam Hadhari has been apprehensively received. The careful and slow way in which information about it has been disseminated reveals something about the awkward intentions of the whole exercise. The 10 principles that Datuk Seri Abdullah presented in his speech at the Umno general assembly last month are strikingly nondescript. Indeed, they are reminiscent of constitutional phrasings, and it may be this inoffensiveness that will make it acceptable and applicable in a worldwide Muslim context.

The most interesting aspect mentioned in Islam Hadhari is that about the mastery of knowledge. Apparently, knowledge in the fields of mathematics and the natural sciences is what Datuk Seri Abdullah is thinking about, especially given the fact that the recent reinstatement of English in Malaysian schools is limited to the teaching of these very subjects. However, the crux of the conflict between science and religion in modern governance does not lie so much in the natural sciences as in the social sciences. How these latter fields of knowledge will be encouraged is what needs to be focused on in the future.

The Prime Minister expressed the view that 'the Malays must have a global mindset, understand the global scenario and be able to face the challenges of the global environment'. This point is markedly different from that of Tun Dr Mahathir, who in 1983 sought cultural change through the emulation of East Asian countries, the values of which he simplified into good work ethics, loyalty to state and company, putting the group before the individual, appreciation of efficiency and excellence, and good management.

Not only was Tun Dr Mahathir's 1983 programme secular and group oriented, as opposed to Datuk Seri Abdullah's strategy, it was not informed by religious terms. It is this fusion of material goals and religious integrity that makes the latter's discourse a solution on both the domestic and international fronts at the same time, aimed at diffusing perceived tension between Islam and modern economic life.

For the promises of the first year to be fulfilled, and for the rhetoric to gain substance, the Prime Minister will need in his second year to be seen as more definite in creating an administrative culture that does not tolerate corruption. Other issues needing immediate attention definitely include the problem of illegal migrants, criminality, rising prices, and the alarmingly inferior quality of infrastructure projects.

Furthermore, a more comprehensive agenda for the structuring of the Islam Hadhari discourse must include concrete measures within the educational system that will direct the Malay mindset more towards self-reliance, science and creativity.

Speaking before the United Nations' General Assembly last month, and in his opportune role as the year's chairman for both the 57-member OIC and the 116-member NAM, Datuk Seri Abdullah talked at length about the importance of multilateralism in international affairs, and of the concerns of Muslims.

At the Oxford Centre for Islamic Studies in Britain at the beginning of the month, he proposed Malaysia as a forum where Muslim and developing countries could resolve conflicts. Where Islam is concerned, he sought increased trade and service transfers between Muslim countries, and open discourse on Islam with Islamic scholars from all over the world.

There are therefore good reasons to assume that the strategy of Datuk Seri Abdullah's regime arches unbroken from a programme for Malay advancement in skills and knowledge, national inter-ethnic peace if not harmony, and Islam's renaissance as a flexible and knowledge-seeking civilisation, all the way to a closing of ranks among Muslim states.

Economic reasons are of course not secondary to religious reasons, the two actually being aligned with each other in Datuk Seri Abdullah's initiative. At the Second OIC Business Forum held in Kuala Lumpur earlier this month, for example, he suggested the food market and the financial sector as areas for Islamic economic cooperation that Islamic unity could lead to.

There are clear reasons why the name Hadhari - civil - has been chosen for this agenda. Its ambitions are both national and global, and their success actually lies in how well they can be understood within the ruling party, by the Malays, among Malaysians at large, and by the world community.

First published as "Abdullah's steady approach wins respect", in Review, *Straits Times*, 30 October 2004. Reproduced with the kind permission of Singapore Press Holdings.

4

'Queuing the crowd' strikes at the heart of corruption

DATUK SERI Abdullah Badawi's government starts off its second year with quick measures to rectify stalled government projects, handle corruption within Umno and in society at large, repatriate illegal immigrants and control traffic offences.

The apparent lack of confidence that the public has immediately shown towards most of these measures is largely due to their ad hoc nature. The types of issues being dealt with are revealing in themselves and are a reality check, providing some understanding of why a new prime minister in a country like Malaysia has to put so much emphasis on raising educational levels and changing mindsets.

It is characteristic of national advancement today that the various arms of government function in accordance with clear rules and regulations that are flexible enough for the handling of new problems. This structure provides all parties, especially the common citizen, with a sense of security and legal predictability.

However, it is most vulnerable to corruption at the executive end. Unreliable enforcement turns the strongest political will into wishful thinking. That is why bureaucratic and police corruption is a more serious matter at the street level than political immorality is. In fact, an efficient executive arm would also work against political corruption.

In this respect, one may differentiate between a queuing society and a crowding society.

So-called advanced nations tend to be legalistic in character, and daily life is highly ordered and routinised. Their peoples are good at queuing, because queuing does get them to where they want to go while crowding does not.

Less standardised nations, on the other hand, tend to be marked by unmediated negotiations and the individual seizing and making of opportunities. There, crowding - jumping the queue - is culture, and effective. This is best observed in traffic. On the road, risk-taking no doubt reaches irrational levels, but that is largely an extension of a general social condition where queuing will not get you far, and where crowding - jumping the queue and being upfront where chances may be found - is to be preferred, and is in fact in most other daily contexts rational.

Rules can be bent, and are often bent. On-the-spot fines for bad traffic behaviour, without corresponding measures to make roadside payoffs by offending drivers impossible, raise issues of legality and fears of increased police corruption.

Making enforcers also judges cannot be wise, or constitutional. A tighter noose makes bribery more attractive on both sides. As long as the system can be beaten, dramatic anti-corruption measures cannot have a lasting effect.

One can approach the question of corruption either as a moral question or as a pragmatic matter. In the former case, one must assume that corruption is sufficiently distinguishable from honest governance, in which case all corruption, no matter how it is defined, is wrong.

In the latter case, corruption is wrong because it undermines the workings and the wealth of the state and of society, in which case it is best defined through its economic and political effects.

Electoral contributions are therefore generally not considered wrong if there is enough consent, silent or otherwise, among voters that they are necessary and that they will not overly influence political policies after the elections. Such contributions reach astronomical sums in advanced democracies. Sophisticated and established channels for supporting candidates financially will therefore facilitate acceptance of electoral contributions, while unsophisticated and ad hoc methods are more easily classified as corruption.

As far as governance is concerned, corruption is bad because it undermines trust in the system. I will queue if it gets me somewhere, and I will jump the queue if I can get my errand done more speedily that way. When corruption is admitted by the government to be a problem, be it in Malaysia or anywhere else, it is also an admission that it is entrenched. Weeding it out will require strong herbicides. Weak concoctions will merely nourish it.

The datuk epidemic that has reached painful levels in Malaysia, with both shiny and shady characters contending to deserve or buy a datukship, is another expression of this beat-the-system syndrome. The entrenchment goes far beyond the failing mechanisms of government to infect the social culture itself, encouraging a mindset that understands crowding to be more rational than queuing.

National development is also about exclusion.

Illegal immigrants crowd national queues that are already threateningly vague and unstable. As with domestic maids, we need these people but we do not want to include them in our exclusive queues. This ambiguity makes control extremely difficult, where labour is sold without basic rights being guaranteed. Mistreatment of the disenfranchised cannot but harden the country's socio-economic environment and must lead to an increase in violent and desperate crimes.

For standing in line to be something that people find worthwhile doing, the legal and bureaucratic mechanisms handling queues must be effective, transparent and responsible.

Queues are boring things, admittedly, but they are the surest symbol and guarantee of fairness and transparency modern societies have. The possibility of jumping the queue is the genesis of corruption. Therefore, in a historical sense, governments can best quell the mob by queuing the crowd.

Having said this, we must also ponder the question whether a queuing society is what we want, and if not, how we can attain a society that is honest yet not regimented.

First published in Review, *Straits Times*, 23 November 2004. Reproduced with the kind permission of Singapore Press Holdings.

5

Time for Umno
to rise above ethnic politics

THINGS THAT succeed become one of two things. They either face irrelevance or they continue their existence as an unquestioned configuring backdrop. Normally, they do a bit of both, because success is often only partial.

Political relations between ethnic groups in Malaysia had already taken the form of ethnic bargains in the early 1950s. It proved to be a successful way of winning independence, given the conditions of the day. Ethnic relations were fragile, British decolonisation was caught up in damage control and the local communists had taken to armed resistance.

The Malayan Chinese Association (MCA) was founded with much encouragement from the British, both to provide the local Chinese with a political alternative that was not obviously tied to Mainland Chinese politics and to create a Chinese-supported partner for the Malay-supported United

Malays National Organisation (Umno). Independence was aided by such a clearly defined inter-ethnic structure.

Following the elections and riots of 1969, the power balance between the ethnic groups and their political representatives veered strongly to accommodate what came to be called the Malay Agenda. Government policies after 1971 were all configured strongly by the programme of the Malay nationalists to advance the socio-political and socio-economic role and status of the Malay community.

The expansion of the ruling Alliance coalition to become Barisan Nasional (BN) also meant a strengthening of Umno's hegemonic status. This also meant that the MCA's status and influence were weakened.

In many ways, this New Economic Policy succeeded. This is commonly described through the welcome emergence of the Malay middle class and the Melayu Baru. Although the NEP ended in 1990, it lived on in practice and in policy in various forms.

However, privatisation and the radical changes in the foreign policy discourse of the Mahathir years, together with the overall economic success of the decade preceding the 1997 to 1998 financial crisis, altered the conditions for inter-ethnic relations.

A broadly held wish to move beyond ethnocentrism as the decisive political and social discourse became more and more obvious throughout the later Mahathir period. The rise of non-governmental organisations intimated that ethnocentric politics were diminishing in importance.

This trend gained dramatic expression when former deputy premier Anwar Ibrahim's refusal to disappear quietly from the political scene in September 1998 served the population with suddenly increased public space. Despite his subsequent removal from the scene, the 1999 general election saw Barisan Alternatif give Umno and the BN a sobering wake-up call.

Apparently, it was Parti Islam SeMalaysia (PAS), and not its partners Keadilan or the Democratic Action Party, that gained decisive ground. This also signalled that Malaysian politics had now become largely an intra-Malay matter.

Since then, Umno, pragmatic and flexible as always and somewhat aided by the political aftermath of 9/11, has regained both the political and moral high ground from PAS in all the states except Kelantan.

The March 2004 general election gave the BN, Umno and Datuk Seri Abdullah Ahmad Badawi the largest mandate it had ever had, with PAS the main loser.

The shift from inter-ethnic balance to Umno hegemony over the years thus led to Malaysian politics becoming centred on intra-Malay leadership, and by extension, to the issue of Islamisation. What this has led to, where non-Malay politics are concerned, is the marginalisation - or the ironic de-politicisation - of ethnicity-based Chinese and Indian political parties and their politicians.

The success of Umno has not led to its own irrelevance, but to the irrelevance of its partners in the erstwhile politics of symmetric ethnic balance.

This can be observed in the discussion now underway in Malaysia about the MCA's present and future role. Picking up on the debate that had been running in Malaysian Chinese newspapers since October, last's month's *Aliran* magazine joined the fray with articles by Mr Francis Loh and Mr Tan Lee Ooi calling for the MCA to return to politics.

No doubt, being an ethnicity-based party in a political scenario where all references to ethnicity and religion are sensitive could not have been easy, and must have left the MCA paranoid and limp.

The strategy that it seemed to have developed over the years was to leave high-power politics well enough alone and to concentrate on economics in its wider contexts, which of course included education. The founding of Universiti

Tunku Abdul Rahman in 2002 and MCA's present Lifelong Learning campaign attest to this.

Perhaps it would be wiser to let the MCA submerge itself into civil society where it can do some tangible good. In a BN where Umno reigns supreme, the MCA lacks the ambition to be anything other than what it had become - 'an extension and instrument of the state so as to assist in maintaining the status quo and in supplementing the delivery of public works and services', as Mr Loh put it.

The political trend, as has been argued, is in favour of issues transcending ethnicity. This in itself is a result of the success of the Malay Agenda, which was aided to some extent by global dynamics. The apparatus of ethnocentric politics - or at least the ethnocentric tenor of the establishment - is showing signs of irrelevance and should perhaps be allowed to remain a backdrop.

Tellingly, even the Islam Hadhari initiative started by Umno under Datuk Seri Abdullah in January last year avoided any mention of ethnicity.

Given the power it presently enjoys, a responsible tactic for Umno to adopt as part of a long-term policy would be to transcend ethnocentric politics on its own, and perhaps even transform itself in the process into a party for Malaysians, and not only Malays.

First published in Review, *Straits Times*, 4 January 2005. Reproduced with the kind permission of Singapore Press Holdings.

6

After the honeymoon comes dialogue

DURING A honeymoon, one does not raise demands or ask for promises made before the wedding to be kept. However, once daily life takes over, so to speak, once things are back to normal, attitudes change. A judging eye replaces the adoring eye, and the possibility of domestic squabbles becomes very real, even imminent.

The end of Datuk Seri Abdullah Badawi's honeymoon with the Malaysian people has been declared many times over the past three months, most recently by his son-in-law Khairy Jamaluddin at the Regional Outlook Forum organised by the Institute of Southeast Asian Studies in Singapore on Jan 6.

To be sure, the wedding had not been posh. It was quiet, and Datuk Seri Abdullah entered into his new relationship with the Malaysian people in a markedly sober fashion. This was a welcome change for many who had grown weary of Tun Dr Mahathir Mohamad's contentiousness. Datuk Seri Abdullah's first year had therefore been appropriately full of reassurances, conciliatory overtures and damage control.

His trouncing of Parti Islam SeMalaysia (PAS) in March last year, together with the continual proselytisation of Islam Hadhari as a platform for Islam and the Malays to engage in modernisation and extra-Malay relations, was certainly reassuring for ethnic minorities and nervous neighbours such as Singapore. His offer to the Muslim world to use Malaysia as a base for religious discussion and Muslim entrepreneurship was also welcome. His overtures to the neighbour across the Causeway to put differences aside, to move into a new period of warmer relations and to harvest 'low-hanging fruits' drew happy and concrete responses from the Singapore Government and private sector. Singapore's investments in Malaysia last year have consequently been many, huge and dramatic.

Datuk Seri Abdullah's attempts to stop the excesses of the Mahathir regime, especially certain last-minute contracts given to certain favourites, have been loudly applauded.

His promises have been as many as they have been welcome. While it is true that it is now time for him to deliver, it is equally true that the biggest promises take the longest time to fulfil, and the end result, even if reasonably successful, might not be especially dramatic.

In truth, Datuk Seri Abdullah had been working on his honeymoon, and travelling a lot to promote Malaysia's image and businesses. The enviable economic situation today testifies to that, as do the good working relations that have been cultivated with neighbours and the world. Malaysia is having a more peaceful time now than it had experienced for quite a while.

This relaxed period may, however, be the lull before the storm, or the silence before the demands. For a relationship to last, explanations must be offered if misunderstandings are to be avoided. Disappointment is a more lasting state than anticipation is. Therefore, given the fact that Datuk Seri Abdullah prefers gradualism to publicity, he needs to maintain a constant dialogue with his people if they are not to misunderstand him.

In this light, the parliamentary committees that he has outlined to collect feedback on important matters are promising. Last July, one was formed to gather reactions to proposals for increasing police power in the face of worsening criminality and for stemming terrorism. In December, another was constituted to collect ideas from various quarters to counteract the disturbing process of ethnic segregation, or lack of national integration.

More publicity and open discussions about such interactions between his regime and the politically maturing Malaysian population would not hurt the country's image and development.

So, after the honeymoon, comes the 'living together' bit. Here, mutual respect and understanding, which are reliant on sincere dialogue, are essential. Communication has to be as direct as possible, with both sides being as free with their views and worries as possible. News heard through the local and global grapevine tends to be distorted and is not conducive to domestic peace.

Since this dialogue is with the masses - the Rakyat - a cacophony of voices is to be expected. Today, when the overseas edition of China's People's Daily (Renmin Ribao), is allowed to circulate in Malaysia, there is no reason why local potential such as Malaysiakini.com should not be granted permission to launch a weekly current affairs journal. Mutual respect requires that both parties consider the other capable of acting maturely, even in presenting, understanding and reacting to diverse views.

There is some symmetry when campaigns for the Rakyat to learn common courtesy, such as that launched by Datuk Seri Abdullah on Tuesday, are matched by campaigns against governmental corruption. Both will take time, and at the end of the day, courage and a willingness to change are required of all involved.

In cases when promises cannot be kept - sometimes this happens despite the will being sincere - then comprehensive explanations must be given and understanding sought. With sufficient mutual respect, things can change for the better when pressure is exerted from above and below at the same time.

First published as "No more sweet talk, it's time to deliver", in Review, *Straits Times*, 13 January 2005. Reproduced with the kind permission of Singapore Press Holdings.

7

Interfaith dialogue
need not be destabilising

IT WOULD seem a given thing in a country where inter-ethnic relations are as thoroughly balanced and institutionalised as in Malaysia, and where the ethnicity of the majority group, the Malays, is strongly defined by religious affinity, that a stable forum is created for discussing issues that otherwise may lead to misunderstanding among Malaysians of different faiths.

The multi-religious make-up of Malaysia is undeniable. Apart from the majority Malays, most other groups are not defined through religion.

According to figures from the 2000 census, Muslims form 60.4 per cent of the population, 19.2 per cent practise Buddhism, 9.1 per cent Christianity, 6.3 per cent Hinduism and 2.6 per cent Confucianism, Taoism, and other traditional

Chinese religions. Baha'i, Sikhism and animism make up the rest.

Now, as the country develops and most citizens experience the insecurities of modernisation and urbanisation, the need to feel secure on civil and religious matters becomes stronger. Discussions between and among people of different religions, and a wider understanding of the implications of the religious practices of others, given Malaysia's diversifying social atmosphere, are undeniably needed.

The recent raid by the Federal Territory Islamic Department (Jawi) on a popular club in Kuala Lumpur led to many public debates that showed how Muslim individuals and groups differed in their views on the matter.

Further controversy is now brewing following a concerted call for the setting up of 'a statutory interfaith body of an advisory, consultative and conciliatory nature for the protection and promotion of peace and harmony'. Many Muslim individuals and groups chose to boycott the two-day national conference in February on the matter, although it was opened by the Minister of Culture, Arts and Heritage, Dr Rais Yatim.

While the minister understood the conference as a rare effort at bringing various faiths together and commendably asked for more open-mindedness from parties concerned, bodies such as PAS Youth chose to condemn the proposal for an interfaith commission, while a coalition of Muslim non-governmental organisations boycotted the conference altogether. Last year, the Allied Coordinating Committee of Islamic NGOs (Accin) had already declared its opposition to the formation of an interfaith body and its intention to boycott discussions related to the proposal.

Prime Minister Datuk Seri Abdullah Badawi, perhaps reacting to rumblings on the ground, advised against the proposal being forwarded since it 'can have an impact on the prevailing religious harmony among people of diverse religions'. Of course, one may think that if such a commission is to be founded, then the best time for it would be when religious harmony prevailed.

However, the terrain is tricky, and the fear is that an institutionalisation of inter-religious dialogues will be perceived as too strong a challenge to Islam's status within the Malaysian state.

Datuk Seri Abdullah's fear of rocking the boat is given an uncomfortable slant by Deputy Premier Datuk Seri Najib Abdul Razak in his muffling reminder that Muslim religious sensitivities should be considered.

Dr Abdullah Mohamed Zin, Minister in the Prime Minister's Department, had earlier in the week claimed that an inter-faith commission would contravene the Federal Constitution.

The proposal for a commission, drafted with the Human Rights Commission of Malaysia as model, was presented to the national conference on Feb 24-25 by a committee led by the Bar Council.

The chairman for the steering committee, Mr Malik Imtiaz Sarwar, sees the formation of the interfaith commission as part of 'the challenge of establishing a mature, liberal and accepting society in which Malaysians of all colours and creed are free to practise and profess their customs, cultures and religious beliefs'.

Datuk Seri Abdullah has, since taking office in 2003, been promoting the perception of Islam in its civilisational mode, and not merely in its sanctioning role.

This programme goes into high gear this year. The sailing will not be plain, or the idea of Islam Hadhari would not have been needed at all. The knowledge-seeking characteristic of his progressive Islam requires dialogue with all interested parties, and while it may be true that such dialogues need not be institutionalised, they do need accessibility, regularity and integrity to be effective.

Currently, the Malaysian Consultative Council of Buddhism, Christianity, Hinduism and Sikhism is the most established interfaith body, but without the participation of Muslims, the 'i' lacks its dot, as the Swedes would put it.

During his visit to the Oxford Centre for Islamic Studies in Britain in October last year, Datuk Seri Abdullah, perhaps moved by the moment, offered Malaysia as a forum for open discourse on Islam with Islamic scholars from all over the world, and as a conflict-resolving centre for Muslim and developing countries.

Hopefully, in the coming months, his vision of a civilising and civilisational Islam will convince more within the country that Malaysia is becoming strong enough and stable enough for unconditional discussions to be possible.

First published in Review, *Straits Times*, 3 March 2005. Reproduced with the kind permission of Singapore Press Holdings.

8

Understanding
post-Mahathir Malaysia

THE FOCUS of political analysis in Malaysia since Tun Dr Mahathir Mohamad handed the reins of government to Datuk Seri Abdullah Badawi has been on how well the latter will do on his own engine, and how well he will limit the excesses of his predecessor. However, beyond studying and commenting on the processes of post-Mahathir politics, Malaysian analysts face a much larger challenge. Tun Dr Mahathir held the country's top position for 22 years. But even before that, he had been influential in Umno politics and directing Malaysian policies. This dominance has been profound in many areas.

   His legacy therefore goes far beyond popularly discussed phenomena such as the Look East philosophy, buying British last, positioning Malaysia as an anti-Western power, industrialisation, privatisation, concentration of power, favouritism as nation-building strategy, his visions of future grandeur, his many deputy prime ministers and his mega-projects.

For historians, journalists and political scientists alike, what remains to be done is a revisit to Malaysia's early history. Especially in its finer points, the period immediately preceding that under a sustained leadership should be studied for trends dismissed deliberately or inadvertently by political agendas. These necessarily constitute a major source for analytical and policy-making inspiration in the post-Great Leader period.

Tun Dr Mahathir had his hits and misses. His longstanding influence on Malaysia's political life could not but have precipitated certain excesses on society in general, and on knowledge creation in particular.

There has been a recent renewed interest in Malaysia's formative years. Books on the subject include Cheah Boon Kheng's Malaysia, The Making of a Nation and Khong Kim Hoong's Merdeka! British Rule and the Struggle for Independence in Malaya 1945-1957. Cheah's book places the first four prime ministers within a comprehensive process of nation-building. Khong's book describes some of the important factors in Malaysian politics.

These works may, along with others, be seen as some of the first initiatives to put the overpowering Mahathir era in the wider context of the nation's history and future.

Beyond such attempts, what is required of Malaysia analysts, given the fact that the country is in a post-Great Leader period, is an awareness of the side effects of Mahathirism. Things highlighted by Tun Dr Mahathir necessarily threw other phenomena into the shadows, and it is the latter that need to be identified.

His stance against the West, for example, excessively influenced the way Malaysia and Malaysians saw (and see) themselves vis-à-vis the world at large. His wish to put

Malaysia on the global map involved the country not only in unnecessary battles of words with bigger powers, but also in a civilisational - and not only national - positioning involving 'the West', 'East Asia' and 'the Muslim world'. His excluding regionalism was conceived within such an ideological context. Notwithstanding the merits of his perspective, a side effect of it was the subsequent detachment of Malaysian foreign policy from the realities of neighbourhood politics.

Since Tun Dr Mahathir's retirement, the concrete reality of Malaysia's neighbourhood tensions, to an extent by coincidence, has made itself felt with a vengeance. Relations with Thailand have recently been damaged by irredentist tensions in that country, while ties with Indonesia deteriorated drastically when Malaysia laid claim earlier this month to disputed islands in the Sulawesi Sea, inopportunely at the same time as Indonesian illegal workers were being rounded up throughout the country. The Indonesian mass media took the opportunity to incite nationalistic passions that were uncomfortably reminiscent of the Konfrontasi of the early 1960s.

These events suggest that a sustained effort to improve ties and cement good relations had been lacking. Indeed, the absence of a deterioration in ties over the last decades should not be mistaken for a bettering of ties.

Datuk Seri Abdullah's efforts immediately after taking office in October 2003 to improve relations with Singapore were a wise remedy prescribed quickly to cure the ignored state of neighbourhood politics. It should be recognised as another of his attempts to rectify the excesses, misses and detrimental side effects of the Mahathir regime.

His battle against corruption, his decision to stop mega-projects wherever possible, his many charm trips to countries around the world, and even his propagation of Islam Hadhari (moderate Islam) and moral behaviour, may all be seen in this light as well.

The salience of such domestic issues should encourage revisits to the 1950s and 1960s by scholars and journalists to search for forgotten trends, and should lead to reassessments of events such as the Baling Talks or May 13, and renewed interest in central personalities such as Tunku Abdul Rahman and Dr Ismail Abdul Rahman.

Datuk Seri Abdullah's policy of investing in agriculture also serves to highlight a phenomenon overshadowed in earlier times. Not only did the New Economic Policy, despite its clear goals, fail to eradicate poverty, but Tun Dr Mahathir's obsession with the creation of a formalistic Malay middle class also logically put all other Malay classes into disfavour.

One should, of course, note that Tun Dr Mahathir, to his lasting credit, did sometimes try to rectify the detrimental side effects of earlier federal policies. His decision to reintroduce English as the language of instruction in the teaching of science and mathematics was most probably prompted by the evident advantage that Asian countries where English is encouraged, such as India and Singapore, obviously possessed in the new economy era.

Thus, behind the Mists of Mahathirism, more inspiration for new perspectives and new possibilities on Malaysian politics and society should be available for those willing to look for it.

First published as "How to understand post-Mahathir Malaysia", in Review, *Straits Times*, 19 March 2005. Reproduced with the kind permission of Singapore Press Holdings.

9

How slow can one go?

SOME CHANGES come about slowly, while others do not happen at all unless at high speed. Given the state of Malaysian Prime Minister Abdullah Badawi's political power, where support for him is enviably large among the people in general and weak within his own party Umno, he must understandably play a balancing game.

In the quest for necessary institutional changes, he must be seen by the general public to be steadfast and decisive, and by party leaders to be conservative and cautious.

This is no easy task, and needless to say, a form of strategy has come about that must, in different ways, please both the party's top and society's bottom. Despite the difficulties this engenders, much has nevertheless been accomplished.

The Malaysian economy is healthy and developing despite an acute lack of labour - and amid growing speculation on the fate of the currency. Ties with Singapore have improved beyond anyone's dreams, while relations with Thailand and Indonesia, despite border tensions, have stayed cordial. In addition, Malaysia's status in the world community remains high, even rising in the West. Indeed, Datuk Seri Abdullah's Islam Hadhari initiative - despite the vagueness of its concept - seems to be receiving wide recognition, even within the Organisation of Islamic Conference.

There is indeed a lot to be said about the efficacy of Datuk Seri Abdullah's slow and steady style of politics. However, what may be required of his administration in the later part of his mandate is the ability to switch gears when needed.

Poverty is being recognised as a vital issue needing comprehensive measures from the government, as is the lack of integration - or perhaps disintegration of relations - between ethnic groups. The Ninth Malaysia Plan, due to start next year, is expected to dwell equally on hard economics and soft intercultural issues.

However, many of the stubborn problems that the government faces are of a structural nature, which means that unhesitant and dramatic measures are required in many areas. The fight against corruption is one example. If corruption can really be eradicated slowly yet surely, then it would have been merely a minor problem to begin with, which it is not. But as former Prime Minister Mahathir Mohamad has lately said - in his defence against claims made in a column in The Star newspaper that he did not do enough to fight corruption during his time in office - what is being dealt with is a culture of corruption. Such a thing is surely flexible enough to parry or absorb any series of soft and slow measures thought up by the government.

The reliance of large numbers of bumiputera firms on government contracts spells systemic weakness. This has been making it difficult for the Prime Minister, who is also Finance Minister, to keep to his plan to successively decrease the budget deficit. Apparently, cutting down on government spending immediately threatens to put many of these enterprises out of business. Thus, economic sense comes into direct conflict with political expedience, a clear sign of a structural flaw.

The international role that Datuk Seri Abdullah's administration has been seeking for Malaysia over the last 20 months straddles both the moderate Muslim world and the powerful East and South Asian economies. In order to attract investments from the one and trade opportunities from the other, domestic politics must be stable and yet dynamic. To achieve this, the state must remedy structural weaknesses quickly and yet smoothly.

These weaknesses include: an educational system where excellence is not of decisive value, entrenched poverty, graduates going unemployed, the dual problem of a lack of labour and illegal migration, widespread corruption, the steady reversal of socio-cultural integration, the separation of the private and the public sectors along ethnic lines, and prolonged inter-ethnic distrust.

Given the strong support that the Prime Minister personally enjoys among the people, what his reforms need are serious involvement from various organisations, and professional support from all ranks of the civil service. This would lessen his reliance on politicians within his own party, and embolden him for his tasks ahead. In fact, manifest popular support would make opponents within the ruling party think twice about withholding support.

The Royal Commission report on the police was released last month, and was generally welcomed as a commendable attempt to deal with the problem of police corruption. Many groups came out in praise of it, although some understandably remained skeptical. Nevertheless, many did engage themselves, offering the authorities ample advice on the matter. This initiative serves well as a focal point where civil society and individuals at large can show open and concrete support for the government. With the hopes of so many now raised, the authorities will feel irresistible pressure to deliver on their promises. More similar events will be needed in the months and years ahead.

The more gears the 'car of state' has at its disposal, the greater its ability to adapt to speedy and unexpected global changes. Some changes must occur slowly, and some must occur swiftly.

First published as "Slow or Fast? Abdullah needs to be nimble with reforms", in Review, *Straits Times*, 11 June 2005. Reproduced with the kind permission of Singapore Press Holdings.

10

Umno should look within
– not at PAS

AS IS to be expected, Malaysia's United Malays National Organisation (Umno) party is keeping a close eye on the Islamic opposition, Parti Islam SeMalaysia (PAS).

But this is more than just a governing party keeping tabs on the opposition. Umno is interested in how its most powerful electoral competitor intends to reform and position itself for the next general election.

However, it may profit Umno more if it looks more closely at itself - as many within the party are urging.

Has Umno much to worry about from PAS? The shock of the 1999 election, when the opposition showed broad gains, has not been forgotten by the ruling Barisan Nasional coalition, of which Umno is the leading party.

After all, it lost oil-rich Terengganu state to PAS. But in hindsight, those results were very much a consequence of the Anwar Ibrahim trial and the fallout from the Asian financial crisis. When it came time for last year's election, with the economy back on track, Terengganu just as surely returned to Barisan Nasional control.

The 1999 election did not so much highlight the opposition's strength as reveal the ruling coalition's weaknesses then.

Now, a year after the 2004 electoral shock, PAS has started to make changes to its leadership line-up. The key question is what options are open to the new non-ulama, or non-cleric, leaders.

PAS' present position on Islam lies far beyond what is normally termed 'moderate', and is in stark contrast to the image presented by Prime Minister Abdullah Ahmad Badawi through Islam Hadhari.

With the installation of new leaders - a de facto takeover by the professional class - changes are afoot in PAS. These will lead to a softening of its religious profile. Indeed, we will see PAS elbowing onto Umno turf.

PAS will certainly become more moderate, and it will launch new initiatives to 'modernise' its brand of Islam - to make the party more acceptable to more Muslims and to convince non-Muslims it is a moderate alternative political force. Without this, no viable Barisan Alternatif, or alternative coalition, with or without Mr Anwar, will appear.

All that notwithstanding, one has to ask to what extent PAS' changes warrant institutional reaction from Umno. The 'Abdullah factor' - the PM's popularity - still carries weight.

Moreover, Islam Hadhari has shown enough promise for Umno to keep promoting it to profile its Malayness and the country's adherence to moderate Islam.

At the same time, the Malaysian Chinese Association (MCA) appears to be going through its own renewal. More than 80 division heads elected recently in preparation for national party elections in August are new. Many of the old guard who survived did so on slim margins.

Such a change - rare for the MCA - reflects strong sentiments on the ground. The MCA is one of Umno's major partners in the ruling coalition, and this generational change should make Umno feel more confident that the coalition is well positioned to withstand opposition challenges.

Nevertheless, given accusations of corruption and impropriety, Umno is under more internal than external pressure to clean up its act.

Recently, as many as 70 of Umno's old (and not so old) guard, led by former deputy premier Ghafar Baba, urged the leadership to stop the erosion of democratic practices in the party. Money politics, they fear, will erode Umno from within to such an extent that it will jeopardise the well being of the country.

So in the end, it matters little whether PAS reforms or not, and if Umno's partners are reliable.

What Umno needs most is to keep an eye on itself. If its house is in order, it won't much matter how others are re-arranging theirs. But if it isn't, then it has cause to worry, no matter what PAS or any other party does.

First published in Review, *Straits Times*, 25 June 2005. Reproduced with the kind permission of Singapore Press Holdings.

11

Shoring up the support pillar

TRYING TO get Musa Hitam out of the way of then-Malaysian Prime Minister Tunku Abdul Rahman's wrath in 1969, Umno leaders, at the suggestion of Ghazali Shafie, apparently requested Sussex University in Britain to give a scholarship to the offending 'young Turk' to study there for a year.

The idea was for him to stay away from Malaysia until things calmed down, following the harsh attacks Musa and some other Umno members had made on the Tunku. The latter included Mahathir Mohamed, who had openly criticised the premier. But as things stood then, it was too late; his expulsion from the party was practically assured.

Records show that Sussex took a while to consider the request. Such a grant was not a given thing, even when requested by a foreign government.

What is interesting about the event, in the light of the free flow of money within Umno and Malaysian politics in recent years, is that Umno leaders in those days did not seem to have had access to ready money, even to finance such a simple procedure, and according to most accounts, would not have made use of it even if they had.

Malaysian politics was indeed different then. Personal integrity was much more appreciated as a political asset in those dedicated days.

Apparently, the reason why a critic like Musa Hitam was shielded was that intra-party criticism was generally accepted, and leaders such as Tun Abdul Razak and Tun Dr Ismail, despite their dislike of the way criticism was being voiced against the Tunku, did not wish the party's young to be discouraged too much from speaking their minds.

Umno has continued ruling Malaysia as the definitive party within the ruling structure of the Alliance and later the Barisan Nasional. The country's transition from a poor agricultural state to an economically respectable nation over the past 35 years has been enviable in many ways.

However, a question that needs asking - an issue that has far-reaching implications - is exactly how this transition has affected the moral fibre, democratic structure and political representation of what was once a party strongly rooted to the ground.

That Umno is riddled with scandals and shadows of scandals, and that its history since 1969 has been filled with dramatic conflicts, show that its adaptation to this transition has been far from satisfactory. Money politics, a term now being surpassed by the officially sanctioned 'political corruption', has left the reputation of the party in worse shape than before.

How this state of affairs in turn mirrors the established workings of the socio-economic structure is a question that needs immediate analysis. Are we dealing with the tip of an iceberg, or can we continue thinking of it as the whole rotten apple?

Things have deteriorated to such an extent that some among the party's old guard have been worried enough to write open letters urging its present leader Datuk Seri Abdullah Badawi to carry out profound changes.

This latest initiative is being led by none other than the 80-year-old former Deputy Prime Minister Ghafar Baba, once the premier-in-waiting. His memorandum, supported by more than 50 Umno veterans, was handed over to Datuk Seri Abdullah at the Kuala Lumpur International Airport late last month.

However, Datuk Seri Abdullah's response was rather lukewarm, if not dismissive. He said: 'I regard the memo as a reminder to me to ensure the success of (the party's programmes). I have no problem with it. If those are their views, then we may assume that they agree with the actions being taken.'

Interviewed in Kuala Lumpur last week, Ghafar Baba explained that Umno is and always has been the pillar of Malaysia, and if that pillar is allowed to decay, the nation as a whole would suffer for it.

He said: 'Chinese friends ask me how Umno is doing. Now why do they worry about Umno? They are not members. The thing is, even they know that Umno must remain strong and sound if the national economy is to continue growing. If anything bad happens to Umno, the country will collapse and businesses will collapse.

'That is why we must stop money politics. There is no doubt that if it continues, Umno will go into crisis. Corruption will become even more rampant. I am sad indeed that this is happening to my country, to my party.'

The ageing statesman worries that the prime minister may not realise how bad things really are, and that yes-men around him are feeding him the false idea that things are rolling along at a satisfactory and effective pace.

He suggests that more direct and interrogative methods are required. 'We have to advise and criticise the government. That is the least we can do. Things are not in a healthy state. The way they are thinking of curbing money politics now will not work.'

There is much talk - and even some action - in Malaysian politics today, for parties to reform and revive themselves. These parties include the mighty Umno, whose internal battles over the past few decades have been occurring within a political economy undergoing tremendous changes.

With wider affluence among the Malays, and among Malaysians in general, the old structure of politics naturally suffers strains. It needs a restructuring - a deconstructing and then reconstructing - of its main supporting pillars.

First published in Review, *Straits Times*, 28 June. 2005. Reproduced with the kind permission of Singapore Press Holdings.

12

A case for tension between state and Umno

MALAYSIANS ARE finally reacting against institutional failings that arose from former Prime Minister Mahathir Mohamad's style of national development. With his retirement, the logic for many of his policies has weakened, a process furthered by his successor Abdullah Badawi's push to limit mega-projects and fight graft.

Within the dominant party, Umno, money politics is just one of many ills whose origins can be traced to Tun Dr Mahathir's one-sided implementation of the New Economic Policy (NEP).

The NEP had two aims: eradicating poverty and increasing employment opportunities for all Malaysians; and accelerating the restructuring of Malaysian society to correct economic imbalance. The ultimate aim: to reduce and eventually eliminate the identification of race with economic function.

According to an official mid-term review of the Second Malaysia Plan (1971-1975), the policy would 'ensure that no particular group experiences any loss or feels any sense of deprivation in the process'.

Tun Dr Mahathir chose to focus on the creation of a small and wealthy class of Malays. Given that the Chinese were hitherto wealthier, this would, statistically at least, enhance income equality between the races.

The fight against poverty was left to take care of itself. The hope was that if the economy grew fast enough, and if the trickling down of wealth from the newly created class was generous enough, the twin goals of the NEP would yet be met.

Such a belief in this process of wealth distribution has proved overly optimistic.

The creation of a small and wealthy class of Malays involved the rationale that their individual well-being and that of their ethnic group strongly overlapped. What was good for one chosen Malay was good for Malays as a whole. For the chosen individual, the ethical need to help in wealth distribution within the Malay community, which was the reason for his advantaged position in the first place, was minimised.

Putting the NEP on this fast track also meant the dismantling of many of the checks and balances that had been in place. The concept of integrity for institutions and individuals alike was diluted. Notions of public ethics became blurred.

Corruption is more than the mere act of buying one's way, or taking payment to help someone buy his or her way, to the front of a queue. It involves individual values being eroded in the absence of public constraints.

Twenty-one months into the new administration, we are beginning to see widespread reaction to this untenable state of affairs. Prime Minister Abdullah recognised that budgetary imbalances had to be brought under control along with the mega-projects. He has had some success in curbing public spending, although the increasing need to cut back on government subsidies is threatening to push inflation upwards.

Now with the second Umno general assembly during his period in office under way in Kuala Lumpur, the mood has been set by recent successes against corrupt practices and by civil society's continuous calls against decaying public morality.

Parliament's Public Accounts Committee recently raised questions about the giant PSC Naval Dockyard's failure so far to deliver any of the offshore patrol vessels it was contracted in 1998 to produce in a deal worth RM5.4 billion (S$2.4 billion). Former Malaysia Airlines officials may be questioned over allegations of illegal practices concerning a cargo contract from 1999 that involved losses of millions of ringgit.

These and many other incidents are signs that things are finally moving on a broad front to remedy alleged excesses of the past and reinstate institutional values needed for good governance to become a national culture.

Malaysian politics has always centred on Umno, making its annual general assemblies a major focus for observers searching for signs of how the constellations of power are developing. This is due largely to the steady reduction of tension between party and state - Umno is increasingly being identified as the state. As such, electoral success in the party is said to be a quick way of securing a government position. Alongside this, money politics and accusations of money politics have become tools of the game.

Lately, the party has been taking these accusations seriously, as evidenced by the formation of a disciplinary board to deal with money politics. There is also mounting pressure from the lower ranks on the party's top people to do more to stop corrupt practices within the party

After the recent suspension of Umno vice-president and Federal Territories Minister Isa Samad, hopes were raised of a clean sweep of high-flying culprits.

Interestingly, when the idea for the Putra World Trade Centre that houses Umno's headquarters was hatched in 1971, the chairman of the committee initially charged with the project, Tun Dr Ismail Abdul Rahman, who was also the Deputy Prime Minister and Minister of Home Affairs, made it a point of principle that it was not to be built on government land. His ideal was that the party and the state had to be kept separate at all costs.

Both Malaysia and Umno may have changed a lot since then, but it is still vital to the moral and political health of the country - in fact of any country - that the tension between state and party is revived and retained. A reliable structure of checks and balances would be hard to screw into place otherwise.

The time may finally be right for Datuk Seri Abdullah to acknowledge the support he has among the lower ranks of his party and among Malaysians in general, and respond confidently with a comprehensive strategy that identifies the root causes of corruption and poverty as being part of past policies that have run their course. Such a strategy can be incorporated into the Ninth Malaysia Plan, whereby institutional flaws within Umno, in the corporate world, and in governmental bodies can be recognised and rectified.

First published in Review, *Straits Times*, 20 July 2005. Reproduced with the kind permission of Singapore Press Holdings.

13

A new Malaysian storyline

THE GENERAL assembly of Malaysia's ruling party, the United Malays National Organization (UMNO), attracts the attention of everyone interested in the past, present and future of the country's politics.

However, Malay culture as such is highly political, and this means that the speeches of Malay politicians and the choices of discourse they make are also rhetorical to a large extent. This makes it difficult for analysts to distinguish the static from the message. What is the cake and what is the icing?

For example, during the 2004 general assembly, the first over which Abdullah Badawi resided as party president, his coinage of the phrase "Towering Malay" (a skilled, successful and devout as well as secular and open-minded Muslim) gained the attention of the mass media. At the 2005 meeting, it was the turn of his deputy premier, Najib Tun Abdul Razak, to play the political word game. His term "Glocal Malay" (Malay with a global mind) captured the imagination of the official media, if not that of the people. Malays form slightly more than 50% of Malaysia's 23 million people.

Ethnic Chinese are the next largest racial group with 22% while Indians form another 7% of the population

Last year, UMNO Youth, which has a self-adopted mission to amplify the basic goals of the party, chose to focus on "The Malay Agenda". This term has the advantage of suggesting continuity and unfinished status with regard to what UMNO sees as the desires of the Malay community. At that meeting, rising star Khairy Jamaluddin was booed, which must have been rather disturbing for a young man with high ambitions.

This year, the youth wing decided to call for a "revival of the NEP", the New Economic Policy implemented in 1970 to help the Malay community gain a higher level of participation in the modern economy. Officially, the NEP ended in 1990, replaced in name, if not in essence, by the National Development Program. One could argue that it somewhat changed in essence the following year when then Prime Minister Dr Mahathir Mohamed announced his view of Malaysia's future - Vision 2020. The focus on quantitative goals was replaced by a concern for qualitative status.

This year, the leaders of UMNO Youth - including Education Minister Hishammuddin Tun Hussein, son of former premier Hussein Onn, one of his deputies, Mukhriz, son of former premier Mahathir, and Jamaluddin, the son-in-law of the current premier - all pushed for a return to the NEP. Since the NEP was never dismantled, this left many confused. What they could have meant, given the fact that the beginnings of meritocracy are being implemented in the educational system, is a return to intake quotas at the tertiary level, and of course to a concentration on quantitative goals, such as the 30% equity ownership by Malays. This time, no one booed Khairy - he has obviously become an accomplished

UMNO politician and might even be ready to go for the UMNO Youth leadership at the party elections in two years.

The 2005 meeting occurred in the shadow of the battle over Approved Permits (APs) for the import of luxury foreign cars, which was ignited by the battle of words between Mahathir, who is now an unpaid adviser to the national car Proton, and his erstwhile supporter, the Minister of International Trade and Industry Rafidah Aziz. This quarrel was partly egged on by Badawi's decision to force the release of the list of AP receivers. Since this was a sudden reversal of his earlier stand not to bow to public pressure, the timing of his change of mind was naturally seen by many to be politically motivated.

This impression of Badawi's increasing pro-activeness was strengthened by the strange absence of Mahathir from the assembly. In the midst of all this, China decided to unpeg its currency. As countless experts had suggested over the past year, the Malaysian ringgit was bound to follow suit. This indeed happened. However, the speed with which this was done added to the impression that Badawi was indeed a man who was now fast gaining real control over the party and the government. That will remain one of the lasting impressions from the 2005 meeting. However, this may only be a supplementary saga to what is more possibly the main story.

While Badawi promised more meritocracy, UMNO Youth appealed for more affirmative action. This "good cop, bad cop" scenario led very quickly to reactions from Chinese leaders from within the ruling coalition to call for a more efficient NEP, and for failures to be identified and rectified.

No doubt, these reactions should be understood in light of the party elections that the Chinese-supported parties within the coalition Barisan Nasional (National Front) are having this month. Nevertheless, this entreaty for a systematic and monitored implementation of the NEP is given further credence by the fatigue Malaysians currently feel about dubious practices by people in positions of power. Money politics, gambling debts, corporate corruption and haughty behaviour by politicians add up to a widespread longing for clean government.

Badawi also drew attention to the harsh pressure exerted by the global economy, which was limiting Malaysia's economic policies. This, together with the initiatives that have been taken immediately after the general assembly by his regime to energize the Association of Southeast Asian Nations (ASEAN) and to further Asian regionalism, may be the cue for how the future of Malaysian politics is to unfold. This is captured in the new phrase New National Agenda (NNA) - a tentative compromise between the ideals of the Malay Agenda and the reality of the global pressure that Malaysia must deal with. Hopefully, Malaysia is realizing that it must abandon its long-held fixation with inter-ethnic relations, and instead adapt to the reality of external forces.

First published in *Asia Times Online*, 9 August 2005. Reproduced with the kind permission of Asia Times Online.

14

Affirmative action part of economic progress

AFFIRMATIVE ACTION programmes have been around in Malaysia since before independence in 1957.

It was obvious to most leaders - British, Malay or Chinese - that the rural Malay population needed systematic and sustained government assistance in order to shift from a colonial economy to an eventual national economy.

The creation of the present ruling party, the United Malays National Organisation (Umno), in 1946 in Johor state was the very result of Malay fears regarding the implementation of the Malayan Union, which they saw as a high-handed and uncomprehending attempt to create a sociopolitical system in which they had little or no say.

The rationale for the party's existence became even clearer when party members resisted founder Onn Jaafar's attempt in 1950 to open up the party to non-Malay members. Despite his practically unassailable position, he was allowed to resign. More than that, he became Umno's major opponent after the British and the communists.

Tunku Abdul Rahman of Kedah state came to power because his expressed views then strategically contrasted greatly with Datuk Onn Jaafar's, and personalities that became vital to the status and success of Umno, such as Tun Dr Ismail Abdul Rahman of Johor and his elder brother, who was a very close friend of the Tunku, Suleiman, joined, partly because they had not trusted Datuk Onn Jaafar, and partly because they agreed with the Tunku's plan for full independence.

The party soon managed to develop into a grassroots representative of the peninsular Malay, even as talks with the British for independence went on alongside the battle against the Malayan Communist Party's (MCP) armed insurgency.

The formation of the Malayan Chinese Association (MCA) in 1951, encouraged by the British, was a tactical move to draw Chinese support away from the MCP.

An *ad hoc* decision in Selangor in 1954 by the Umno and MCA branches there to build a coalition proved to be highly successful and was implemented throughout the peninsula.

The Alliance idea was intuitively attractive and easily assimilated by the population - each race being represented by its own party, with these parties working together in a coalition for independence and nation building.

This led to the astounding electoral victory of 1955. By then, the communist insurgency was losing its momentum and the British finally had no reason left to not agree to full independence.

However, the general idea that the Alliance was a successful solution was shown to be incorrect by the time of the elections of May 10, 1969. As home affairs minister Ismail himself was to say in a closed-door speech to Alliance members in January 1971, the euphoria following Merdeka meant that the Alliance could not be challenged in the 1959 elections.

The MCA leader at that time, Mr Lim Chong Eu, attempted to gain a larger allotment of seats for the party from the Tunku, and failed. The Alliance idea was not without its problems.

The Alliance victory in the 1964 elections, Tun Dr Ismail went on in that honest and revealing speech, was very much due to the fact that the country was fighting Indonesian aggression at that time.

The ending of the Indonesian *konfrontasi* in 1966 meant that Malaysian voters and Malaysia - now minus Singapore, which had to leave in 1965 for reasons of differences in management of inter-racial relations, strategy of nation-building and clashes between leading personalities - had to deal with internal tensions that had been building up since the 1950s.

Ten years after independence, the question of language became critical. The deal made with the British was that English would be the main language until 1967, after which Malay would take over, with English playing a supporting role.

Apparently, the troubles since 1957 had meant that this deadline was not taken seriously by many of the parties involved, and their preparation for this shift had therefore been ineffectual and practically non-existent.

By the time election campaigning got under way in early 1969, tensions were so high that no punches were pulled in the language used and the issues raised in the political speeches.

Victory rallies by the opposition parties on the three evenings following May 10 infected the inter-ethnic atmosphere even further.

The rest is history. Riots broke out in Kuala Lumpur on May 13 that put nation building on a new course. What was amazing was how quickly the Tunku was pushed to the side by these events. The dynamics of Malay politics required that he take full blame for the breakdown in the apparent inter-ethnic peace.

Emergency rule was declared, and the retired home affairs minister, Tun Dr Ismail, was called back by the new man in charge, the Tunku's deputy Abdul Razak bin Hussain. The trust he enjoyed with the different races was sorely needed by the times.

Over the next four years in his country's history, Tun Dr Ismail was to play a decisive role. There is little doubt that he did his job well. Within two years, the new regime felt secure enough to reopen Parliament.

However, in reaction to the unhampered campaigning for the May 10 elections, the Constitution was amended to make discussions of certain 'sensitive issues' illegal.

The New Economic Policy (NEP) that grew out of the mayhem of those days was a rational piece of work. Its main weakness was the concentration on quantitative goals. This may have been a sign of the times and of how most experts of the period were wont to think. Architects of the policy, such as Tun Dr Ismail, were conscious of the long-term dangers of such a comprehensive affirmative action plan. He considered it a handicap programme not unlike that found in his favourite sport - golf - and he made certain that a time limit of 20 years was put on it.

The golf handicap idea suggests why the NEP goals were as quantitative as they were. However, what is also significant is that incessant training is required for improvements to be made, and there is a definite system through which these improvements are measured. One works towards getting rid of the handicap. Thus, the NEP succeeds by making itself irrelevant.

One must not forget that the NEP is an economic policy. It tried to balance the goals of sustaining endless economic growth, diminishing the income gap and ending the correlation in real terms between race and class.

Furthermore, it was a compromise between the ambitions of the 'ultra' Malay nationalists within Umno and the moderates.

Outside Umno, compromises were attempted in the aftermath of the MCA's failure to deliver the Chinese vote in the formation of the Barisan Nasional to replace the Alliance.

What is important to remember here is that while the NEP was rational and compromising, the atmosphere throughout society at that time was not. This had a sad impact on how the NEP was understood and accepted. While the Malays saw it as the spearhead of a racial victory, the Chinese saw it as a racial loss. Few saw it the way some of the policy's architects had wished, namely as a national development programme; this is despite the fact that the NEP was best presented within the Second Malaysia Plan (1971-1976).

While an economic policy has a time span, a victory - or a loss - does not. It is this difference in understanding what kind of phenomenon the NEP is that has configured much of inter-ethnic relations in Malaysia since then.

The political architects of the NEP died early - Tun Dr Ismail in August 1973 and Tun Razak in January 1976. The influence of Tun Dr Mahathir Mohamed - someone who in this context was once seen as an 'ultra' but who later became a 'moderate' - was therefore to have a heavy impact on how the NEP was to develop and be implemented.

While the external policies of the Razak regime aimed for neutrality during the Cold War, Tun Dr Mahathir quickly moved his economic rhetoric towards a nationalism based on an East-West orientation. Economic growth became the NEP's main focus, and mega-projects were explained via a Keynesian logic of governmental economic stimulation.

Malay progress *vis-à-vis* the non-Malays was reduced to the formation of an urban Malay middle class. Poverty was left to fend for itself, and the government relied on a trickling down of wealth to help the wider population.

The 1990 limit on the NEP came and went. Tun Dr Mahathir changed its name to the National Development Programme but would soon after introduce his Vision 2020. What was significant about this shift was that the quantitative goals were exchanged for qualitative goals, and more importantly, this shift involved a movement from an inter-ethnic focus to a Malaysia-in-the-world perspective.

The downside of Tun Dr Mahathir's fast-track development was the fact that the trickle-down effect was weak and the authoritarianism of the times enhanced a culture lacking in accountability, lacking in an understanding of maintenance and sustainability of gains made, lacking in transparency and riddled with corrupt practices.

As his successor has said, the toughest job he was saddled with was getting the budget deficit under control. He is nevertheless trying, and along with his promise to fight graft on all levels, call for increased meritocracy and relative success in depoliticising Islam in Malaysia, there exists a new atmosphere in the country.

Some mistakenly take this atmosphere to mean the end of the era of affirmative action programmes. This is far from the case. Meritocratic values are not necessarily opposed to affirmative action. The analogy of golf tells us that.

What is required instead, and what is increasingly possible given that Malaysians nowadays tend to locate themselves within a world economy and not in an inter-ethnic domestic paradigm - as evidenced by the country's many global initiatives such as the East Asian Summit, to be held in Kuala Lumpur in December - is an implementation of affirmative action programmes built on mechanisms of accountability and performance management.

The Malay Agenda must now take global dynamics into consideration. This is what is being witnessed, and the apparent tension at the 2005 Umno general assembly between a revival of the NEP and the call for meritocracy has been balanced within the idea of a New National

Agenda. This not only allows for a new lease of life for measures to help the Malays, but perhaps can also get all Malaysians involved in it through best practices based on transparency and efficiency.

Affirmative action programmes should not be mistaken for social welfare programmes. The latter are needed as humane measures and socio-political necessities to aid those who cannot fend for themselves. The former are part of the game of economic progress. They will be useful until they become unnecessary.

However, affirmative action programmes can succeed only if their efficiency is measurable. This requires transparency, the involvement of all parties regardless of racial affinity and, most importantly, it must lead to the self-sustainability of achieved goals.

First published in Review, *Straits Times*, 10 August 2005. Reproduced with the kind permission of Singapore Press Holdings.

15

Inter-ethnic unity
needs political cooperation

WITH THE change in its leadership at party elections last weekend, the Malaysian Chinese Association (MCA) now faces the task of convincing the Chinese community in Malaysia that it can renew itself and regain relevance as its main political representative.

It has been given a chance to do this sooner than it might have wished for.

At the general assembly of the United Malays National Organisation (Umno) in July, the leadership of the youth wing of this major party of the ruling coalition decided to call for a revival of the New Economic Policy (NEP).

This comprehensive affirmative action policy was introduced in 1970 and ended officially in 1990 to be succeeded by the National Development Programme (NDP) between 1991 and 2000.

Something called the National Vision Policy (NVP) took over in 2001. Besides the ending of quotas on intakes into tertiary institutions, nothing substantial changed along the way.

These acronyms are in many ways the popular articulation of more concrete developmental measures subsumed under 'Malaysia plans'. The NEP covered the Second to the Fifth Malaysia Plans, while the NDP reflected the Sixth and Seventh, and the NVP expressed the Eighth.

Apparently, it is for the purpose of putting a popular term on the Ninth Malaysia Plan starting next year that the New National Agenda (NNA) has been coined.

This new acronym is purportedly meant for articulating the many programmes to be implemented in the next 15 years during which Malaysia will make its last-ditch attempt to achieve developed status for the country.

The subject matter of the major speeches at the Umno general assembly revealed a tension between the needs of Malaysia's domestic politics on the one hand and that of international economics on the other.

Malay rights and the continuation of affirmative action programmes were proclaimed at the same time that the citizenry was warned that the government's options were becoming increasingly limited.

The MCA leadership judged Umno Youth's challenge too glaring to ignore, especially when a tough party election was just around the corner. Its retorts have centred on the idea that the major problem facing Malaysia is not whether the NEP should be revived or not, but rather the need to face up to the facts concerning its many failures.

This appears to be a reasonable standpoint. What threatens to lead to unnecessary aggravation and heated arguments is the assumption among many that the country no longer has the resource or the time needed for affirmative action programmes at all. Meritocracy does not always contradict affirmative actions, however, and the admission on all sides that the NEP did not succeed as it should have on all fronts in fact tells us that many of the conditions that made the NEP necessary - in the opinion of most Malay leaders - are still relevant.

The 'Spirit of the NEP' that is so often mentioned needs to be defined. In principle, it was the acceptance of compromise - among the major political parties following the 1969 riots - around the idea that Malay economic backwardness had to be remedied to a significant extent, and that this was to be done with the help of all parties, and within a growing economy.

As with all compromises, some heavy arm-twisting may have been exercised. Be that as it may, Malaysia has lived with it for 35 years, and, indeed, it seems reasonable at this stage for the major parties concerned in the original NEP to look at alternative routes of development that the NEP could have taken.

This may help as a reminder about what the original motives were, and perhaps in time the decades of digging in to defend ethnic interests, and the distancing between races in order to keep the peace, may become unnecessary.

New processes can be constructed, which adopt more sophisticated ideas about performance management, monitoring, accountability and result maintenance, and put to good use. Open discussions about how affirmative action programmes should be implemented in the future certainly do not amount to a denial of the need for them. In fact, that need is taken most seriously when it is most openly discussed.

The New Automotive Policy that is to be announced by the Prime Minister in September will be a good indicator of what the Abdullah administration hopes to accomplish with the NNA. Even more information should be forthcoming when the Cabinet reshuffle expected to be made before the start of the fasting month in October is actually carried through.

Apparently, Umno Youth has agreed to discussions with component parties within the ruling National Front. This is largely in response to proposals by two of its major partners, MCA and Gerakan, the latter of which is having its party elections this weekend. One can but hope that these discussions are allowed to be held as between equal and trusting partners - at an essential round table - and not within a 'big brother, small brother' context.

What Malaysia no longer has resource and time for is a continuing denial that serious inter-ethnic political cooperation is a prerequisite for inter-ethnic unity and national integration. Compromises are not forever. They may be adjusted when found to be inefficient or unnecessary, and as quickly as possible.

First published in Review, *Straits Times*, 26 August 2005. Reproduced with the kind permission of Singapore Press Holdings.

16

Debate can help define history

EARLY THIS month, a lively and heated debate broke out in Malaysia between the opposition Democratic Action Party or DAP, and the youth wing of the leading party in the ruling National Front coalition, Umno. This debate may actually encourage a better understanding of Malaysia's early history.

What apparently got things started was an article posted on the website of the DAP on Sept 1. Provocatively titled The Real Fighters for Merdeka, it was authored by the party's international secretary, Mr Ronnie Liu Tian Khiew.

The new deputy leader of Umno Youth, Mr Khairy Jamaluddin, quickly took issue with Mr Liu's claims. Mr Khairy took Mr Liu to task for not recognising Tunku Abdul Rahman as the father of independence, and for apparently crediting the communist party led by Chin Peng for pressuring the British to grant Malaysia independence.

Mr Liu denied the charges, although he admitted that his formulations may have been clumsy, and called for a public debate on the matter.

Mr Khairy's simultaneous challenge to one of the DAP leaders, Mr Lim Kit Siang, to a parliamentary debate was easily parried by the latter, who referred to the many occasions throughout the last two decades when he had shown great public respect for the Tunku as Bapa Malaysia, or Father of Malaysia.

What began as a war of words soon turned pictorial, so to speak, when Umno Youth on Sept 9 put the cover of Chin Peng's book, My Side Of The Story, on its website, superimposed with a portrait of Mr Liu alongside leading opposition figures such as Mr Lim and Mr Karpal Singh of the DAP, former deputy premier Datuk Seri Anwar Ibrahim, Kelantan Mentri Besar Datuk Nik Aziz Nik Mat and Islamic party PAS' chief, Datuk Abdul Hadi Awang. The whole was accompanied by an incomprehensible heading: Komunis selamanya (forever communists).

The matter had by then become a legal issue. Deputy Minister of Internal Security, Datuk Noh Omar, announced the same day that the police had initiated investigations into Mr Liu's article under the Seditions Act.

Meanwhile, the DAP's national legal bureau lodged a police report in Sitiawan against Umno Youth's retouched cover, claiming that it amounted to criminal defamation under the Printing Presses and Publications Act of 1984.

A few days later, Umno Youth leader Datuk Hishamuddin Hussein announced that he was having the offending 'cartoon' removed from the homepage. DAP secretary-general Lim Guan Eng responded by promising to do likewise with Mr Liu's article.

For the time being, the website war seems to be on hold.

What remains is what it tells us about the state of Malaysian politics and, more importantly, the state of Malaysia's understanding of its own history.

Every nation has its favourite stories about its origins. Britain has the signing of the Magna Carta, the reign of Elizabeth I, the Battle of Trafalgar - the relevance given to each decided by the individual storyteller's aims. Alongside these, it also has the Arthurian myths.

China has its Yellow Emperor, the First Emperor of Qin, and so on. Sweden has the all-conquering Gustav Vasa; the United States has its founding fathers, the Boston Tea Party and the ride of Paul Revere; and France and Russia each has its revolution, among other events.

The new Central Asian nations that arose after the disintegration of the Soviet Union look to details from the conquest of Genghis Khan for their origins.

By its very nature, the line between fact and mythical glorification can never be clear. It is the stuff of national history to identify events and personalities as pivotal points in the development of the nation's identity. This simplification is necessary for public consumption. In fact, it is the essence of the national story.

So when Umno Youth attacked Mr Liu's account, the major concern was that it would lead to 'confusion among the people', as one official put it.

Histories of national genesis decide ontological unquestionability. Such projects will always find voluntary gatekeepers who do their job by discouraging reassessments of early national history. While iconic history may aid national cohesion, it does so by denying fullness of being to the events and personalities involved.

That said, the latest tiff between the DAP and Umno Youth does point a finger at some major issues that Malaysia needs to appraise.

The comfortable familiarity with British ways that Malaysia's founding fathers felt, and that Mr Liu thought diminished their status as 'real freedom fighters', can just as easily be turned around as proof of the wisdom of the military adage of Sun Tzu that deep knowledge about one's opponents is necessary for success, and that the real hero succeeds to the extent of avoiding warfare.

What has seemed to be a useless conflict among conventional opponents can start processes that bring positive and long-term effects. The former inspector-general of police, Tun Hanif Omar, now a columnist for The Star newspaper, for example, responded in an article on Sept 11 that discussed the post-war years of Malaysian history in great detail and without slamming doors on other interpretative contributions.

Skeletal official history can only gain from being given details - about events and about personalities.

Hopefully, more such debate, even if ignited by narrow political diatribes, will kindle greater interest in the details of the history of Malaysia and its founding heroes.

It is only through such a process that later generations of Malaysians can continue to appreciate the country's many heroes, and perhaps find models from the past to help them become towering Malaysians of the future.

First published in Review, *Straits Times*, 20 September 2005. Reproduced with the kind permission of Singapore Press Holdings.

17

UMNO and the price of success

FEW POLITICAL parties have succeeded in their original intentions as much as Malaysia's United Malays National Organization (UMNO). Since its founding in 1946, it has overwhelmed its opponents to such an extent that its main challenge today is to keep itself sound without external orientation.

UMNO started out as a major reaction among Malays against the British initiative to create a single polity throughout the peninsula - inhabitants independent of ethnic background, and in accordance with the *jus soli* principle, would enjoy equal citizenship rights. This hasty move proved overly insensitive to the feelings of Malays, and was perceived by them as the decisive step in the usurpation of Malay sovereignty.

Under the leadership of Datuk Onn Jaafar of Johor, Malays managed to reject what they saw as a major threat to their natural rights. When Onn Jaafar later changed his mind and proclaimed a vision of a polity that was not race-based, meaning in effect that UMNO was to represent all races, he was allowed to resign.

The lesson was not lost on his successor, Tunku Abdul Rahman, who realized that the very rationale for UMNO's existence - the proclaiming of the notion of special Malay rights - could not be openly abandoned if its leader was to survive. Since this ambition necessarily involved independence from the colonial masters, the goal of national freedom became the party's expressed goal.

With this aim clearly identified, it then became possible for UMNO leadership to work out strategies for wresting control over British Malaya from the British. The armed struggle between the British and the Malayan communists that started in 1948 was partly inspired by world events such as the success of Mao Zedong in China, by the rise of nationalism throughout the world and by the success of the British in curbing communist-inspired union activities in Singapore and Malaya. This made it all the more necessary for the British to deal with nationalist parties such as UMNO and to encourage the founding of others such as the Malayan Chinese Association. The weakened British Empire had recently lost its Indian dominion and was in no position to oppose Malayan independence for too long. The concern for the colonialists - given the stark danger posed by global communism - was to cut losses and to make certain colonies that were about to be lost would remain allies and profitable. This played into the hands of UMNO and its allies, whose leaders possessed sufficient knowledge about the limitations of the British at that time to enable them to develop strategies for a peaceful handover of power.

With the forming of the Alliance in 1955 - whereby each of the three main races within the British Malay territories was represented by its own party, and whereby these parties would later jointly govern the new nation - a compromise was forged that promised sufficient security for the British to grant independence.

And so this came about on August 31, 1957.

Between then and 1969, the Alliance government survived many trials, including the formation of Malaysia, the confrontation with Indonesia (or *Konfrontasi*, a small undeclared war between 1962 and 1966, in which Indonesian president Sukarno tried to destroy the newly created nation of Malaysia), and the separation of Singapore.

However, it did not survive the reforms effectuated after the race riots of May 1969. By 1974, UMNO had persuaded the opposition Parti Islam SeMalaysia (PAS) and the Gerakan (Rakyat Malaysia Party or PGRM) to participate in a larger coalition called the National Front (Barisan Nasional). With that, Malaysian governance entered a new phase. The neat Alliance solution may have worked well in achieving independence, but the realities of the country's post-colonial socioeconomics soon demanded another form of power sharing for stability to be at all possible.

UMNO rose to that challenge, and with the introduction of the wide-ranging New Economic Policy to fight poverty and to end the association of race with economic function, and with the sewing together of a new system of inter-party cooperation, it restructured Malaysian politics forever. In the process, it gained further hegemonic power.

Since then, with some exceptions, political confrontations have largely been within the Malay community. A major split occurred within UMNO in 1987, but the party nevertheless continued to rule. Another challenge to the secular UMNO was the transition it was called upon to make to contain the growing "Muslimness" of the Malays. This it also managed to do, and strategies it adopted included the recruitment into its ranks of vocal Muslim leaders such as Anwar Ibrahim.

The next big challenge it faced was the groundswell of discontent that followed the sacking of Deputy Prime

Minister Anwar Ibrahim (over allegations of sexual impropriety) in September 1998, the forming of the *reformasi* movement and the founding of the Keadilan party. This peaked with the success of the Islamist party, Parti Islam SeMalaysia (PAS), in the 1999 elections when PAS took two states and strongly challenged the government's control over the other northern states.

But again, UMNO rose to the occasion, and under a new leader - Abdullah Badawi - and with the Muslim slogan *Islam Hadhari*, it decisively repulsed the PAS challenge in the 2004 general elections.

The question that now needs to be asked is how UMNO's ability to remain in power has affected its very nature. Apparently, major side effects of UMNO's success include the absence of healthy pressure from outside the party, the rise of intra-party corruption and the lack of control over wealth distribution.

The new challenge now lies within the triumphant UMNO itself. It lacks crucial external help in self-orientation. Indeed, if non-Malay Malaysians were to look the political truth in the eye, they could be excused for wondering whether their best bet for gaining greater political influence is to seek membership in UMNO. UMNO, in turn, would need to negotiate its own transition from being the champion of Malay rights to being the guarantor of Malaysian rights. Open membership would prod other race-based parties to follow suit and allow all Malaysians, independent on ethnic affiliation, to be members as well. That would indeed bring about an even greater change in Malaysian governance.

First published in *Asia Times Online*, 21 September 2005. Reproduced with the kind permission of Asia Times Online.

18

NEP: Never-Ending Programme?

NATIONS WRITE the history that suits them. Be that as it may, they do have a history that deserves objective discussion. Even new nations have to live with legacies of the past, however painful and embarrassing. How power was exercised in the past has to be analysed, because that information leaves the strongest imprint and the deepest influence on the present state of socio-political knowledge.

In the case of peninsular Malaya, colonialism had a relatively lucrative and peaceful time. The gaining of independence for the new nation of Malaysia - and Singapore - was also relatively peaceful.

Unlike countries that came into being through revolution, Malaysia's path towards a future free from the limitations of its past has been staggered and slowed - and its epistemological heritage has not been radically challenged.

Colonialism on the peninsula took what could be called a soft approach, meaning that no bloody military conquest or battle was required. What happened in the Pangkor Treaty of 1874 was that the British managed to start a negotiating process with the sultans for gaining increasing control over the peninsula's resources. The method of control they thought up was the implanting of what were interestingly called 'advisers' in the courts of the sultans.

These men did more than advise, of course. They exercised real power, leaving the sultans with the residual but face-saving right to decide on cultural matters.

As the British Empire encroached further into the peninsula, and the locals were sidelined or incorporated into the colonial administration, their loss of rights and sovereignty gained an automatic camouflage.

The system managed to encourage the locals, who were being sidelined and ignored by the new economy that was gaining more footholds on the peninsula, to think that they were in fact being protected.

Common notions of sovereignty were replaced by ideas of trusteeship. Notions of rights - human rights if you like - and duties were replaced by defensive ideas of ethnicised rights and governmental patronage. This epistemological legacy is what Malaysia still lives with, almost 50 years after independence.

When independence came, it was also a relatively soft affair. As soon as the races showed that they could cooperate, and as soon as the communist threat had been contained, independence was quickly granted. This could have lulled Tunku Abdul Rahman, the first prime minister of Malaysia, into thinking that all was well and that he could take his time in building the country.

Others were not as tolerant as he was, and not as patient.

When things blew up in May 1969, and racial killings took place in the streets, radical measures were called for, the most enduring of these subsumed under what we today call the New Economic Policy, the NEP.

There are a few points that must be made clear about the NEP. Firstly, it was a two-pronged plan: It would eradicate poverty, and it would restructure the socio-economics of the country in the vital sense of dissociating race from economic function.

Secondly, there was a time-span. It was after all a government policy - not a piece of legislation - and had clear goals, and the means of implementation were to be worked out along the way.

Thirdly, in aiding the Malay population, it also had a decolonising function. It would end the sidelining of the Malays from the economic mainstream. This is borne out by the fact that the British were quickly elbowed out of major companies such as Guthries and Sime Darby.

This process is perhaps best expressed by the analogy used by one of the architects of the NEP, the late Tun Dr Ismail, who was deputy prime minister and home affairs minister in the days after the May 13 riots. He used the term 'handicap', as understood in the game of golf, to describe how the NEP was supposed to make it possible for newcomers to play with seasoned players and improve themselves.

What Tun Dr Ismail wanted through the NEP was for a handicap system to be put in place that would inspire the Malays to excel, measure how they excel, and integrate the socio-economics of the nation in the process.

There was however a parallel line of thought among the Malays and within the ruling United Malays National Organisation (Umno) – the so-called 'ultras', the Malay nationalists. For them, the NEP was the substantiation of the notion of Malay Special Rights.

This second line of thought evolved into the bumiputera policy – but 'handicap' was now more a medical term than a notion taken from golf. The handicap – now transformed into a right - is permanent, and so, they argue, the NEP should be permanent. Whenever 'Malay politics' is played today, this line of argument comes into easy use.

What place should affirmative action programmes occupy in Malaysia today?

Affirmative action is arguably necessary because the playing field is never even. However, since such an action has a goal, any affirmative action programme needs to be closely monitored and improvements made where necessary. When it has served its purpose, it needs to be replaced by other measures to remedy other injustices.

A successful affirmative action therefore aims to make itself redundant. Its methods must be constructed in such a way that the goals it achieves must be self-sustaining, and not temporary.

So it must be asked: How has the NEP fared? Has it achieved its goals? Or have its methods strayed? Has it solved the poverty issue, which was one of its original aims? Only when these questions are effectively dealt with can future affirmative action policies be altered to fit the challenges of present times.

Like other nations, Malaysia today faces the myriad challenges posed by globalisation. The competition is now with the economic forces being set free throughout the region and the world. Affirmative action programmes continue to be needed because socio-economic imbalances abound, but to be effective, they must promote cooperation across party and ethnic lines.

As the earlier analysis of colonial history showed, protection was not always protection. This epistemological battle is Malaysia's big challenge today.

First published in Review, *Straits Times*, 14 October 2005. Reproduced with the kind permission of Singapore Press Holdings.

19

Shifting into third gear for his third year

DATUK SERI Abdullah Badawi will have been Malaysia's prime minister for exactly two years this weekend. Although only a week has passed since he suffered the tragedy of his wife's death, he has shown himself to be spiritually strong.

Former deputy prime minister Musa Hitam, a close friend, observed that he remains focused and collected, and he had been well prepared for what seemed inevitable. 'The Malays gain a lot of comfort from the idea of takdir (things being fated), and Pak Lah is a religious man,' he noted.

Datuk Seri Abdullah will go ahead with the Cabinet Hari Raya Puasa Open House next week. This will be held at Putra World Trade Centre in Kuala Lumpur, where the public will, for the second year in a row, have the chance to meet all government ministers gathered at one venue for Hari Raya.

Going into his third year as prime minister, Datuk Seri Abdullah, by all accounts, appears prepared to stay on course, continue his reforms, and exert his power more forcefully.

At the end of his first year, in October last year, at a dinner held in his honour by the mentri besar of Perak, he stated that he had until then been sowing 'high-yielding seeds', and these would soon mature. Patience was what he thought was needed.

From the start, Datuk Seri Abdullah's administration has shown a preference for gradualism in internal affairs and diplomacy in external matters. However, even gradualism can move at different speeds. As the administration goes into its third year, the speed of reforms should increase.

A good indicator is the National Automotive Policy (NAP). The framework for the NAP was announced recently, with exact details to be given in the coming months.

Those who had been waiting for it for signs of future economic thinking saw the realities of the global economy acknowledged, even as the special position the national car maker Proton had enjoyed is to fade away gradually. Nationalist sentiments have to give way to the realities of global forces.

The NAP is a staggered move and wisely constructed, since numerous Malaysians are dependent on the domestic car industry, and any sudden pulling of the proverbial rug from under their feet will hurt. It also staves off criticism that the Abdullah regime is giving in to external forces too readily, or that it is abandoning Proton.

Proton, which had enjoyed a 50 per cent excise duty rebate, will lose it under the new framework, but will be compensated by industrywide incentives.

These will apparently include soft loans and research grants.

The higher the investment in research and development, the higher the grants. Other car makers, such as Toyota, Honda and Nissan, will also benefit from the grants.

The new system will, it is hoped, buy some time for Proton, while nudging it into open competition with other producers.

Neighbouring countries also seem placated by the NAP framework, mainly because it is consistent with Asean Free Trade Area (Afta) agreement expectations and practices.

The NAP, which probably should have been applied years ago, may be the harbingers of how further reforms are to be structured. It also signals that the two-year-old regime, in its slow, steady fashion, does mean business.

It is true that many wish changes could come faster, since faults in the system are so obvious. However, these faults are old and entrenched, and to be fair, the political complexities of Malaysian politics make effective reform a sluggish vehicle to steer.

This is also evident in the continuing speculation about a Cabinet reshuffle. Here, within the workings of Umno party politics, perhaps more than anywhere else, may be found the ropes that bind the Abdullah regime hardest.

Nevertheless, events over the past two years have helped loosen their grip.

The spectacular victory of the ruling coalition in the general elections in March last year was largely due to Datuk Seri Abdullah's personality.

The Islamic Parti Islam SeMalaysia (PAS) was trounced, thanks partly to the idea of civilisational Islam - Islam Hadhari - the prime minister propounded. Mending the psychological split in the Malay voting population was no small achievement.

This was further enhanced soon afterwards by the release of former deputy prime minister Anwar Ibrahim. This raised Datuk Seri Abdullah's stature as a moral man who prefers to be effective behind the scenes rather than through dramatic appearances.

The fight against corruption has had some success, though far from what most think could be possible. The recent resignation of Federal Territories Minister Isa Samad - after he was found guilty of buying votes at the Umno party elections last year - stands out as a lone peak in that battle.

The NAP also contributes towards ending the debate on approved permits (APs), which had been fuelled in recent months by fiery public comments from former prime minister Mahathir Mohamed, and the Minister for International Trade and Industry, Datuk Seri Rafidah Aziz.

In what amounted to strong disapproval of the way APs had been issued by the ministry, Datuk Seri Abdullah decided to handle the matter under the NAP, putting it under the charge of his own office.

Under the NAP, APs are to be granted directly to bumiputera-controlled public-listed companies, and restrictions are put on the import of used cars that are less than a year old. The latter measure is to help plug a loophole by which new cars are brought in as slightly used cars.

The coming Ninth Malaysia Plan - with discussions that will supposedly take place throughout Malaysia to define the New National Agenda (NNA) to guide Malaysia towards the milestone year of 2020 - provides the opportunity for Datuk Seri Abdullah to leave a strong imprint on Malaysia's future development, and to fix its course.

A changed Cabinet, appointed by the prime minister in accordance with the huge popular mandate he was given early last year, and one that understands the importance of government accountability and is more openly dedicated to comprehensive reform, appears the logical thing for Datuk Seri Abdullah to aim for at this point in his premiership.

The construction of "a government that is scientific and not one that acts on intuition", as Tan Sri Musa puts it, would be the ideal.

First published in Review, *Straits Times*, 29 October 2005. Reproduced with the kind permission of Singapore Press Holdings.

20

All eyes on Kelantan by-election

THE DEATH of Kelantan state assemblyman Wan Abdul Aziz Wan Jaafar from liver cancer on Oct 31 has thrown his party, Parti Islam SeMalaysia (PAS), into its biggest crisis since the March 21 general election last year.

Back then, PAS was defeated in neighbouring Terengganu state and almost lost its stronghold of Kelantan.

Wan Abdul Aziz, with a wafer-thin majority of 56 votes, helped PAS - and the opposition in general - to retain control over at least one state and deny Barisan Nasional (BN) a clean sweep of all 13 states in the Federation.

However, with his sudden death, the constituency of Pengkalan Pasir - located just outside Kota Baru - is now up for grabs. With PAS holding only a majority of three (24 seats against BN's 21) in Kelantan, the leadership that was elected in June this year is facing its worst challenge to date.

Not only will the result of the by-election scheduled for Dec 6 be a test of Kelantanese confidence in PAS, it will also show how the new image of a younger and more moderate party being built by its leaders has been received.

Furthermore, it will indicate how well the relatively new regime in Kuala Lumpur has been able to sell its reforms in the Malay heartlands.

PAS is therefore taking no chances. If it loses, its majority in Kelantan will be whittled to one, and that shaky margin can easily be lost through a single defection. No one doubts that BN possesses the means - and the will - to win quick converts.

To counteract the electoral apparatus that BN is putting into place, PAS intends to distribute daily newsletters free to all and sundry. Its women's wing will be knocking on doors and doing what little it can to neutralise the many initiatives that the various Umno wings are taking. Wanita Umno will be mobilising 1,000 of its members, while Putera Umno - a newly formed wing - has announced that an astounding 10 per cent of its members will be called in. If true, this amounts to almost 20,000 people. They will furthermore be accompanied by members of Umno Youth. PAS' youth wing, in turn, is hoping to get 3,000 of its members involved.

PAS' general tactic will be to draw unflattering attention to Umno's reputation, both where electoral ethics and the unbalanced concentration on material advancement are concerned.

What is most dramatic is the fact that PAS has already succeeded in recruiting former deputy prime minister Anwar Ibrahim for its campaign. This has already been officially confirmed by Tian Chua, the information chief of Parti Keadilan Rakyat, to which Datuk Seri Anwar is adviser.

Datuk Seri Anwar, who is currently banned from holding political positions, is expected to turn up on Nomination Day.

His appearances in Kelantan are known for being crowd-pullers, and recent developments that hint of systemic corruption and incompetence, like the huge losses being suffered by prestigious corporations such as Malaysia Airlines and Bank Islam, will provide him with no lack of ammunition.

Not only will this be Mr Anwar's first openly political activity since his release in September last year, it will also be tantamount to the complete closing of all doors back into Umno for him.

This is something he must be painfully conscious of, and his decision to back PAS in this crucial by-election shows that he has chosen a definite path for his political future.

BN smells blood, and is moving in with all the artillery it can muster.

Deputy Prime Minister Najib Razak and Umno Youth's deputy chief Khairy Jamaluddin, the son-in-law of Prime Minister Abdullah Badawi, have separately graced recent Hari Raya events in Pengkalan Pasir.

Datuk Seri Abdullah, who is Umno president as well as BN chairman, has reportedly challenged PAS to dissolve the state assembly if it should lose the by-election.

This uncharacteristic 'arrogance', as PAS vice-president Husam Musa chose to call it, shows how badly Umno wants to win. PAS, on its part, cannot afford to lose because that may very well mean the start of the slippery slope to political insignificance. Datuk Seri Abdullah also plans be visit the constituency to contribute to the campaign.

Umno will be wooing the young, probably using the argument articulated by Mr Khairy that PAS is 'hindering the Malay Agenda'.

The Malaysian Chinese Association has also announced that it will mobilise its people to secure a majority of the 966 Chinese voters involved. These make up 5 per cent of the voter population, and may be the deciding factor in the split Malay constituency.

PAS, in turn, is making full use of Datuk Annuar Tan Abdullah, the only PAS leader of Chinese descent, who is a state executive council and central committee member, to appeal to this group of voters.

Nomination Day is Nov 27. Apparently, PAS has already picked its man. Mr Husam Musa has disclosed that the chosen one is a local personality. Rumours have it that he is former state executive councillor Hanifa Ahmad, a politician born, bred and still domiciled in Pengkalan Pasir.

Umno has at least three names to choose from.

First, there is Pasir Mas division head Datuk Abdul Rahim Abdul Rahman, who contested for Pengkalan Pasir and was defeated in 1999; second, there is his deputy Hanifa Mamat, who lost by 56 votes last year in the same constituency; and third, there is the young vice-chairman Che Johan Che Pa.

As added excitement, Mr Ibrahim Ali, a deputy minister in the Prime Minister's Department until he was sacked after last year's general election for running as an independent candidate, has announced his decision to fight for the vacant seat. He has rated his own chances as 'fair'.

Of further national interest is the fact that Kelantan borders the increasingly troubled provinces of southern Thailand.

As the situation in Thailand gets more and more volatile, Malaysia's federal government will wish to be more directly present at and in control of the border.

Although the Prime Minister has expressly asked that security issues be avoided, his regime will be more than happy to be ruling Kota Baru - surprisingly declared by PAS on Oct 1 as an 'Islamic City' - for defense and for diplomatic reasons.

Pengkalan Pasir will thus be flooded with Umno and PAS people over the coming weeks.

It should become quite clear to the 18,411 eligible voters that the results of their election will stretch beyond local or even Kelantanese horizons.

How they vote on Dec 6 will have great significance for the candidates, for their parties, for the future of oppositional politics in Malaysia, and even for diplomatic relations with Thailand.

First published in Review, *Straits Times*, 21 November 2005. Reproduced with the kind permission of Singapore Press Holdings.

21

Seize the moment
to reform the police

MALAYSIANS CAN be a querulous lot. However, every now and then, they do come to agree on a specific issue. It is during such a time that their leaders have to bear their moral duty and amplify the significance of the issue, and take appropriate political action.

Prime Minister Abdullah Badawi finds himself in the midst of such a time.

The scandal now rising to a boil after the release of a video clip showing a nude female detainee, possibly of Chinese origin, being forced to do repeated ear-squats by a police constable has focused diverse voices in Malaysia into a roar of outrage against the long and unruly arm of the law.

This comes hot on the heels of other shocking complaints about police misconduct.

One recent case involved three Chinese nationals who were stopped at a checkpoint, and on the suspicion that their passports were fake, they were locked up for four nights and peeped at while they bathed. Their documents turned out to be totally in order. After their release, they were harassed at their homes in the middle of the night by police visits.

Earlier last month, four Chinese nationals complained that they were stripped and forced to do ear-squats by a policewoman.

Another case involved a Malaysian being sued by the policeman whom she had reported for corruption after he was freed on a technicality.

Even without the race element, these events are sensitive enough to undermine what trust in the police that the Malaysian public at large had. Before the racial element gains further relevance, therefore, the Abdullah administration has to act, and be seen to act, decisively. More than that, eyes will be observing how the Prime Minister, given his declared agenda of being tough on corruption, will be taking advantage of these developments. Should he, for some obscure reason, allow the dust to settle without gaining ground against the 'culture of corruption' in the public sector, then public confidence in his ability and will to deliver on his promise to create a clean Malaysia will dip, perhaps irretrievably.

The fact that the story broke just as Datuk Seri Abdullah was bound for Malta to attend the Commonwealth Heads of Government Meeting gave it added international coverage. Furious and saddened, he had to call a special press conference in Malta in order to publicly promise decisive action.

It is close to impossible to provide any acceptable excuse for the kind of police haughtiness and sense of untouchability that is being demonstrated, and that many suspect are born of a culture of prolonged and uncorrected corruption.

Both the Prime Minister and his deputy, Datuk Seri Najib Razak, have stated that there will be no cover-up, and the former has reportedly told the Deputy Inspector-General of Police, Datuk Musa Hassan, as much. It is sad that the country's two top leaders have to promise something that should be a matter of course.

Datuk Musa caused further uproar by giving higher priority to apprehending the person who taped the MMS video than to dealing with those who had ill-treated the Chinese woman. It did not help matters that Deputy Internal Security Minister Noh Omar announced on Monday that an internal investigation showed that the police had but followed due procedure. Things were starting very much to smell like a classic cover-up, and a defiant one at that.

In the meantime, loud voices have been raised from within the ruling Barisan Nasional and from without that no further delay in establishing an Independent Police Complaints and Misconduct Commission (IPCMC) could be tolerated. Such a body had been suggested by the Royal Commission on the Royal Malaysian Police in its long-awaited report made public in June this year. Even prior to recent claims of abusive police behaviour, sceptics were doubting aloud whether such a body would ever see the light of day.

The Prime Minister, on returning to Malaysia from Malta on Monday, ordered the immediate setting up of an independent body to investigate the case. Whether or not this body is the embryo of an IPCMC is far from certain.

What many fear will be the end result is that a few individual police officers will be punished in some fashion, after which police business and behaviour will be allowed to return to what has sadly become normal.

No crisis is without its opportunities, though. The political caution that Datuk Seri Abdullah had to exercise in his earlier two years in office is no longer necessary, given the general outrage over this issue.

To retain his political credibility, he must now ride on the widespread public outrage and the broad parliamentary backing being offered him. He now has a heaven-sent chance to reform the police force, from top to bottom. Such an achievement would snowball across the establishment.

These recent events are not significant for the fact that they have hurt both national pride and the image of the police. They are important because they describe in graphic detail the undeniably sorry state of what was once - and could be again - a respected police force.

First published as "Seize chance to reform police", in Review, *Straits Times*, 2 December 2005. Reproduced with the kind permission of Singapore Press Holdings.

22

Umno-PAS polarity
appears to be fading

THE RESULT of the Pengkalan Pasir by-election of Dec 6 did not serve as a good gauge for many aspects of Malaysian politics as many had hoped it would. Apparently, things could have gone one way or the other, leaving nothing definite to be judged from the outcome.

What it managed to show, however, was the overpowering strength of the central coalition. By sheer force of numbers and resources, it countered and steamrollered everything PAS could put together to defend its backyard.

Former deputy premier Anwar Ibrahim's appearance for PAS before an enthusiastic crowd of 10,000 was not reflected in the polling result, which leads one to question how much the voters cared about the vital issues touched on by him, and indeed, how much they actually support him today. Issues he brought up, to loud applause, included corruption in the government, the theoretical weakness of Islam Hadhari, and the dubious behaviour of the Royal Police Force.

How the final result affects Datuk Seri Anwar's future political strategy is unclear. If PAS, or a limited Barisan Alternatif for that matter, cannot suffice in bringing him back to the corridors of power, then the only option open to him is a humble return to Umno. The interesting question then is how he is to gain sufficiently powerful allies within the ruling party.

The fact that PAS had controlled the Pengkalan Pasir constituency since 1990 did not help its campaign either. In fact, the lack of development in the constituency over the past 15 years, for whatever reason, was another argument used by BN that a regime change was in order.

Even independent candidate Datuk Ibrahim Ali, whose anti-Umno campaign hurt BN's chances much more than it hurt those of PAS, could not stop the federal coalition. His 415 supporters probably had Umno as their second choice.

The 56-vote advantage that PAS enjoyed was thus changed into a 134-vote victory for BN, and BN's Hanafi Mamat managed to avenge his loss of the same constituency in the March 2004 general elections.

The Chinese vote must once again be deemed vital to this latest Umno victory. The Malaysian Chinese Association (MCA) put in its own people and resources to maximise the number of Chinese who were registered in the constituency taking the trouble to cast their votes.

Does the final result of the by-election reflect support for Prime Minister Abdullah Badawi's initiatives and actions over the past 19 months since the 2004 general elections? That would be reading too much into too little, although one could reasonably say that no decline in support for his regime is suggested by the result, despite his initiatives and actions. No doubt, the immediacy of bread and butter issues was a more decisive factor than analytical conclusions about them.

While Datuk Seri Abdullah was busy with international issues as chairman of the Organisation of the Islamic Congress and with preparations for the Asean Summit and the East Asia Summit, his deputy, Defence Minister Najib Razak, was entrusted with leading the BN charge on PAS. The success of that expedition put Datuk Seri Najib in the limelight, and will look good on his 'curriculum vitae' when the time comes for him to elbow for the top position in the country.

Controversies still remain about the rights and wrongs of the by-election, and PAS has filed a petition to nullify results, claiming that BN had made inappropriate use of postal votes and recruited "phantom voters" to gain the slim victory.

No overturning of the electoral result is expected to come out of what some see as a 'sour grape' reaction on the part of the loser.

What is most serious for PAS is the fact that its new leadership of young professionals does not seem to have left much of a positive impression on voter sympathy. With spiritual leader Nik Abdul Aziz Nik Mat soon to retire, the party is indeed in dire need of some heavy brainstorming. If a change of personnel has indeed failed to turn around the downward trend of voter support, then a change in policy is required.

More religion in politics does not seem a viable option, given the general global atmosphere. Less religion in politics is therefore the only way left to go.

However, that direction would mean that PAS will soon have to make use of discourses that Umno is more at home with. A PAS that sounds like an Umno Light does not seem a wise position to take.

PAS' impasse suggests that something dramatic is about to occur in Malaysian – or Malay – politics. The religious factor that came into play throughout the 1970s, 1980s and 1990s to mark Malay development and to redefine Malay identity *vis-à-vis* non-Malay Malaysians, has run out of steam.

The Umno-PAS polarity is fading away, and has played its part. What will take its place depends on how the coalition itself develops. The opposition parties seem powerless. A Barisan Alternatif in future elections without the Democratic Action Party (DAP) will not garner enough support to be a real threat. In fact, a return by the DAP to such a mission may spell its own end, given the punishment it suffered from voters in 1999 for adopting common cause with PAS.

Partners in the coalition, judging from past behaviour, will remain disciplined. But at some point, when the Umno-controlled ruling front has succeeded with the help of its institutions and resources in defeating and co-opting the oppositional parties, it will start losing its *raison d'etre*. More correctly, parliamentary rule itself will start losing legitimacy when no voice that cannot be ignored remains outside the governing complex. The BN will then have succeeded in becoming the equivalent of the Houses of Parliament.

First published in Review, *Straits Times*, 15 December 2005. Reproduced with the kind permission of Singapore Press Holdings.

23

Malaysia's thin line between state and faith

FOR SOMEONE who sees gradualism as a political virtue, Malaysian Prime Minister Datuk Seri Abdullah Badawi reacted to the policy memorandum that his non-Muslim Cabinet ministers submitted to him at a Cabinet meeting on Jan 19 with impressive speed.

The nine ministers, following the lead of the religious and legal bureaus of the Malaysian Chinese Association (MCA), had called for a review of Article 121 (1A) of the federal Constitution, which states that civil courts 'shall have no jurisdiction in respect of any matter within the jurisdiction of syariah courts'.

Over 200 protesters held a noisy demonstration outside the National Mosque after Friday prayers on the day the memorandum became public news.

The Prime Minister decided to take a clear stand quickly, and announced on Jan 21 that the piece of legislature in question did not require any amendment.

Surprisingly, it was made publicly known that the ministers had had discussions with NGOs such as the Malaysian Consultative Council on Buddhism, Christianity, Hinduism and Sikhism (MCCBCHS) prior to their unprecedented move. Such open cooperation between government leaders and civil society activists, especially in a public lobby to put pressure on the Prime Minister, is quite unheard of in Malaysia.

However, following the Prime Minister's rebuke, the ministers retracted their initiative. The MCA, a major partner in the ruling front, quickly announced that the matter was settled and that they would obediently do as the Prime Minister wished.

This in itself may not be a surprise, but it nevertheless suggests a lack of conviction about the path chosen a couple of days earlier. What helps explain the sudden change of heart by the Cabinet ministers is the fact that the Prime Minister also promised to review 'subsidiary legislature'.

A couple of days prior to this dramatic turn of events, the Cabinet had unanimously ordered the Federal Territories Islamic Affairs Department (Jawi) to disband the 75-member Putrajaya Islamic Council Volunteers Squad that it had formed a day or so earlier.

Jawi, seeing the compact opposition from above, chose to disband its 'snoop squad'. This matter could have prompted the ministers to go further to seek legal clarity once and for all in a potentially explosive area of Malaysian life.

The latest promises by the Prime Minister that changes were nevertheless a-coming also caused the MCCBCHS, in a responsible show of support, to cancel its newly initiated nationwide signature campaign for a review of the Constitution's Article 121 (1A).

A question begging to be asked: Why hadn't the Cabinet discussed the issue behind closed doors if the sponsors of the memorandum were so willing to retract their tract? Had the Prime Minister been so unapproachable that such a document was needed to get his attention, or was there some choreographed chain of events at the end of which the final results were expected?

As with several other sensitive matters in the federal Constitution, this issue will continue to generate debate - and heat.

While standing behind Article 121 (1A), the federal government cannot afford to allow the syariah court to expand its jurisdiction. After all, its own claim to power rests with the sanctity of the civil courts and their jurisdictional scope.

The historical genesis of Article 121 (1A) goes back to the Pangkor Treaty of 1874 when the British managed to gain administrative power over Perak. By 1895, they gained the same power over Selangor, Pahang and Negeri Sembilan. In Negeri Sembilan that year, it was agreed that the British would provide decisive 'advice' on 'all matters of administration other than those touching the Mohammadan religion'.

Though of colonial origin, the separation of civil and religious administration is what allows the modern Malaysian state to exert political power from the centre in Putrajaya. The Islamisation drive over the past two decades blurred this fact for many.

Malaysia is a Muslim state in that it has a national religion, but it is not an Islamic state, and the guarantor of that is the popularly elected federal government itself.

However, no serious challenge to the legal diarchy can be expected. As suggested by Deputy Prime Minister Najib Razak, any changes made to the Constitution would not change the institutional status of the syariah courts.

One can only speculate about how much the dramatic show of discomfort by the nine non-Muslim ministers influenced the Syariah High Court in Negeri Sembilan last Monday to decide that a Malay woman, Nyonya Tahir (aka Wong Ah Kiu), who died on Jan 19, and who to all intents and purposes had lived her life as a Chinese of Buddhist faith, was to be buried as a Buddhist.

Had the syariah court's decision gone the other way, the Prime Minister would have had to suffer pressure more agonising than a memorandum from basically compliant members of his own Cabinet. Things would most definitely have come to a head.

The case of Nyonya Tahir contrasts sharply with that of national hero Moorthy Maniam, whose burial in December last year started the latest controversy over Malaysia's diarchic court system.

The syariah court had ruled that he had converted to Islam, despite his wife not knowing anything about it, and therefore had to be buried as a Muslim. The wife took the case to court. The Kuala Lumpur High Court ruled on Dec 28 that it had no right to intervene in a matter within the syariah court's jurisdiction. That ruling will apparently discourage Muslims from seeking legal support in leaving their religion, something they are forbidden from doing in Malaysia.

What shocked Malaysian non-Muslims, though, was the fact that the wife, S. Kaliammal, who wanted him buried as the Hindu she knew, could not turn to any civil authority for redress. She and their nine-year-old daughter did not attend the burial ceremony.

Along the path towards 2020, some decisive test of Malaysia's legal maturity has to come, and the diarchic structure has to undergo further rationalisation so that future ambiguities can be avoided.

How the nation passes that test will depend on the preparatory steps the government takes now.

First published in Review, *Straits Times*, 25 February 2006. Reproduced with the kind permission of Singapore Press Holdings.

24

Too much consociationalism for Malaysia's own good

Quite obviously, the Cabinet reshuffle Malaysian Prime Minister Abdullah Badawi announced on Feb 14, was carried out to prepare the regime for the Ninth Malaysia Plan that is to be announced in the coming weeks.

The next five years, despite statistically argued economic progress, will be a make-or-break period for Malaysia.

Despite this, the prime minister chose to be conservative and cautious.

The exercise has left many people perplexed, if not deeply disappointed. Many wonder if the de-Mahathirisation drive has ended before it began giving definite results.

Of course, the process of de-Mahathirisation itself may be but the wet dream of those - and they are many - who believe in the existence of an inherent conflict within the ruling

United Malays National Organisation (Umno) dating from the late 1980s. In the aftermath of the Anwar Ibrahim episode and the edifying Asian Crisis, such a conflict may no longer be as relevant an analytical device as it once was.

The reshuffle shows more than a mere lack of imagination on the part of the premier. It displays a sorry lack of young talents available to him, given the political structure. In any case, the signal sent to investors and voters is not an encouraging one. This does not bode well for the upcoming development plan.

The problems Malaysia faces are far from all being Tun Dr Mahathir Mohamad's creation, nor are all its successes his doing. Therefore, structural changes many hope will come only through a process that can be clearly recognised as de-Mahathirisation will not be enough.

While ridding the leadership of all tainted leaders active during the Mahathir years may give satisfaction to many, finding young talent who enter politics because they care for the future of the country and not because they cannot imagine a better career path, is a tougher and more necessary mission.

The Cabinet reshuffle is perhaps a revelation of how limited the prime minister's options really are, and, more seriously, of how the consociational system has stiffened with old age.

The country is undoubtedly full of eager and brilliant patriots. What limits them is a political system that discourages activism that does not fit consociational politics.

When Datuk Seri Abdullah - a handpicked and not elected leader - swept away the opposition in the general election of 2004, it was a clear sign that his promise of accountability and transparency had struck a chord among voters tired of corruption and confrontational politics.

The least one can say about the past two years is that Malaysian politics has stopped being confrontational, both domestically and internationally. Datuk Seri Abdullah's friendly and quiet style of politics has indeed acted as a balm on the tired nerves of many Malaysians.

However, where the fight against corruption is concerned, few believe that slow style of politics carried on for too long will actually work.

Datuk Seri Anwar Ibrahim, now adviser to the opposition party Parti Keadilan Rakyat, for example, believes Datuk Seri Abdullah, in exercising excessive caution, has thrown away a golden chance, and the struggle to exorcise corrupt practices has been forfeited.

Even if the prime minister truly believes a series of minor but significant changes is the best tactic, he needs to persuade his fellow citizens such is indeed the case. His warning to his ministers that their performance and their words will be monitored hereafter can be taken seriously only to the extent that channels for complaints are made easily available.

The Alliance consociation was highly effective in gaining independence for Malaysia, but socio-economic conditions, ideologies and voter population changes soon rendered that model unusable. The succeeding Barisan Nasional model that today involves 14 bigger parties was developed after the 1969 elections and the subsequent racial riots.

Since all parties in the ruling coalition must be represented in the Cabinet, as well as all Umno state branches plus the federal territory of Kuala Lumpur, Datuk Seri Abdullah has had very few cards in his deck for a reshuffle. The long wait was due more to a lack of options than a lack of inspiration.

Mr Maurice Baker, Singapore's high commissioner to Kuala Lumpur in the early 1970s and a close friend of Tun Abdul Razak Hussein, Malaysia's prime minister at that time, said recently in an interview that Tun Razak once privately confessed his dilemma to him: 'In Singapore, you pick the best of the best and make them ministers, while here, representatives from all the 13 state branches are forced onto me, and I have nevertheless to make the whole thing work.'

Politics is supposedly the art of doing the possible, and what may have been impossible yesterday may have become an imperative today. The question to answer is: How unchangeable is consociational politics, and are the limits logical or merely conventional?

The elusive national unity the country continuously strives for may require that the consociational straitjacket be loosened in stages. In a paradoxical fashion, Malaysia is presently suffering from too much representative democracy.

First published as "Little choice for Abdullah in Cabinet reshuffle" in Review, *Straits Times*, 25 February 2006. Reproduced with the kind permission of Singapore Press Holdings.

On Islam and
Nation Building

25

Adapting Islam
to modern statehood

THE MODERN period saw the serial destruction of civilisations and empires throughout the world. In Europe alone, World War I destroyed at least three long-lived empires.

All over the world, the colonialism that went before and after this event undermined empires and cultures that had configured human existence for hundreds, if not thousands, of years.

In South-east Asia, the Portuguese shattered the Malaccan Empire in 1511 while Ferdinand Magellan claimed the Filipino islands for Spain 10 years later.

In time, the Dutch took control of South-east Asia, while the English settled for India. By mid-19th century, the empires farthest away from Western Europe – Manchurian China and Tokugawa Japan – were falling apart under the threat of European colonisation.

The necessity to react to the multi-frontal hegemony of Western Europe often meant that advanced polities throughout the world had to reformulate their entire socio-political and epistemic heritage to accommodate European trespasses.

Regardless of whether the fall of empires involved colonisation or not, an abrupt interruption of internal dynamics in culture, knowledge construction, politics and economics took place.

The subsequent resurrection of some of these civilisations and empires in the shape of reformed polities is the story of modern times. In some cases, profound changes were enforced, and nations survived even at the cost of what some would call cultural suicide. Japan was such a case. It dismantled its samurai culture to withstand Western hegemony, and succeeded in mounting a formidable challenge to the Western world order until its defeat in 1945. China's route was just as tortuous, and also involved the rejection of central aspects of its culture, such as its classical language and its Confucian philosophy. As part of the bargain, it experienced civil conflicts, cultural revolutions and cold wars. Today, it is apparent that these countries - along with most of East and South-east Asia, and emergent India - have found a workable balance between Western science, culture on the one hand; and the preservation of parts of their traditional culture on the other. The Muslim world as a whole has not been as lucky, and not for lack of trying. Colonialism, as pointed out by researchers such as J.S. Furnivall and Bernard S. Cohn, was always an exercise in epistemic amputation and cultural dislodgement.

The histories of non-European lands were rewritten, leading to a shattering of the wholeness of these regions.

This temporal and spatial loss of orientation dismantled the interconnectedness of the civilisation's surviving parts, and its rationale.

Peoples were left with traditions practised but not connected in their minds as an experienced whole. These societies were left with the obsession of constructing a new rationale and a new integratedness that could help them survive in the global political economy.

Over the last 150 years, the achievement of political stability and economic strength became the criteria for successful civilizational reorientation. This is finally being achieved on a broad front across East and South-east Asia, and with it a promise of civilisational re-rationalisation and a regaining of pride of place in the world.

The chaos now visited on the Muslim world – be it the result of neo-colonialism or the failure of modernisation projects – may to no small extent be ascribed to a failure to end the confusion left by 'civilizational amputations', and the splitting of the Ottoman Empire. It is within such a perspective that the full potential of the newly coined term 'Islam Hadhari' may be realised – the 'civilisation' aspect is of greater importance than that of religion.

The term can be made to express the inescapable post-colonial project of constructing a new rationale to reconnect the segments of Muslim culture left after the period of colonialism.

In this context, forms of fundamentalism may be understood as quick-fix solutions adopted to remedy the condition of being civilisationally cut adrift. If any one of these were to have led to political peace and economic growth, a renewing rationale for the Muslim world would have been born.

This has not happened.

Malaysia, being probably the Muslim country most respected in line with these two criteria, has therefore often expressed the wish to be a living argument that development and the practice of Islam are not at odds with each other.

When Tun Dr Mahathir Mohamad claimed in 2002 that Malaysia was already an Islamic state, he was more than merely declaring the opposition Islamic party – Parti Islam SeMalaysia (PAS) – irrelevant and misguided. He was in fact indicating that his party, Umno, and the Barisan Nasional (National Front) regime that he had led for 20 years, had developed the right combination between modern statehood and traditional Islam. Immediately after taking over the premiership on Oct 30 last year, Datuk Seri Abdullah Badawi launched the 'project' of 'Islam Hadhari'. It took a year before the 10 major principles of this understanding of Islam were made public.

As he claims, the issue does not involve sectarianism or a new understanding of Islam. We may perhaps be seeing an attempt to conceptualise Islam as a civilisation – and not merely a religion – engaged in regaining lost epistemic and cultural integratedness. The criteria for this are, again, political peace and economic growth. Indeed, the perception of Islam as merely religion can be seen as a major result of the civilizational fragmentation mentioned above. The call for Muslim cooperation in the economic and academic field that Datuk Seri Abdullah has made as chairman of the Organisation of Islamic Conference and the Non-Aligned Movement accords with such an agenda. The worsening of relations between the United States and Muslim populations throughout the world, even before the Sept 11, 2001 attacks in New York and Washington, has given cause for more haste among Muslims to achieve a civilisational strategy that works.

Major areas of dynamic interplay between secularism and religion include Islamic banking. It may yet prove to be a beneficial device for Malaysia to bridge the gap between the economic agenda of the regime and the hopes of religious Malays.

Since 1983, when Bank Islam Malaysia Berhad was established, Malaysia had slowly been establishing a framework for Islamic banking. In 1993, an interest-free banking system was implemented alongside the conventional banking system.

A second Islamic financial institution, Bank Bumi Mualamat Malaysia, was set up in 1998, in the middle of a controversial nationwide bank-merging exercise. Together with the setting up of special trust funds for the poor, Islamic banking became a social reality.

In October this year, two Middle Eastern banks – Saudi Arabia's gigantic Al Rajhi Banking and Investment, a consortium led by the Qatar Islamic Bank – were granted licenses to operate in Malaysia together with Kuwait Finance House, which had received its nod in May. Three local banks have also been allowed to engage in Islamic banking, taking the number of Islamic banks in Malaysia to eight. There is thus a continuous trend in Malaysia's development, where material and political imperatives are informed by the religion, the Muslimness, of its majority culture. No doubt, the fact that it straddles more than one civilisational sphere has been a great advantage. Resistance to global forces was a permanent theme under Tun Dr Mahathir, and Malaysia's economic success in tandem with its widespread Islamisation had a significance that was perhaps better understood by him than by his successor.

The Islam Hadhari initiative should therefore be analysed as an important spillover – if not a consciously constructed inheritance – of Tun Dr Mahathir's domestic and foreign policy strategies. The view of nation building as the foundation stone for 'civilizational rebuilding' in the post-colonial period then gains a stark relevance. Malaysia's positioning of Islam within a successful formula built on ethnic bargains and state-driven capitalist development holds promise where a 'renaissance' of the Islamic world is concerned. One should perhaps understand the initiative, not so much as a new presentation of Islam, but as a cautious attempt to discourse a new Muslim – Orang Islam Baru – adapted to the needs of a developing multi-ethnic nation state; and in a larger context, it seeks to regain lost civilisation.

Revealingly, except for the first - piety and faith in Allah - all the goals of Islam Hadhari are matter-of-fact civilizational goals.

First published in Review, *Straits Times*, 11 December 2004. Reproduced with the kind permission of Singapore Press Holdings.

26

Islam as a tool of modernization

A BIG worry in Iraq and the wider Middle East is that Islam and modernization are enemies. But Malaysian history over the past three decades shows that this belief is mistaken. In fact, Islamization has proved to be an effective political means of reconciling the majority of Malays to the country's rapid economic development.

In the early 1970's, when it was still an overwhelmingly agrarian country and Islamization was just gaining momentum, Malaysia embarked on its so-called "New Economic Policy" (NEP), designed to help the majority Malays gain a bigger share of the country's wealth. After three decades of spectacular economic growth, many Malays have become prosperous not only through secular capitalism, but through the country's renewed sense of Islamic identity, one which – for the most part – embraced modernization. (Of course, paradoxes appear every now and then, such as when globalization is advocated alongside demands for stronger censorship.)

Islamic-minded politicians such as Anwar Ibrahim gained prominence when Islamization took off in the 1970's. But the Islam they promoted was not backward looking; instead, it sought to shape a modernizing economic policy that took note of Muslim sensibilities.

Faced with the grassroots popularity of this movement, by 1982 the government of then Prime Minister Mahathir Mohamed decided to co-opt Anwar Ibrahim into his United Malays National Organisation (UMNO), the dominant party within the country's ruling coalition. The strategy worked well, and helped defuse Islamic opposition to the wrenching changes that accompanied the country's rapid economic modernization.

During the 1990's, however, Anwar increased his influence within the party, unsettling many of the old guard. Matters came to a head after the 1997 financial crisis, when Anwar, the deputy prime minister, adopted an even more economically liberal approach then Mahathir. Partly in response to this challenge, Anwar was sacked.

Anwar's bizarre trial and sentencing on charges of sodomy and abuse of power followed the founding of the *reformasi* movement, as growing anti-UMNO and anti-Mahathir sentiments took hold among Islamic-minded Malays. This culminated in poor electoral results for the ruling coalition in November 1999.

The Islamist party, Parti Islam SeMalaysia (PAS), took power in the states of Kelantan and Trengganu and strongly threatened UMNO in other northern states. The personal conflict between Mahathir and Anwar thus led to an apparent rupture between Malaysia's Islamist political forces and the modernizers of UMNO.

So once again, Mahathir felt pressure to adopt a strategy aimed at preventing Islam from becoming a tool of opposition. This impulse strongly affected his choice of a successor when he decided to step down as prime minister. His choice of Abdullah Badawi, the current prime minister, helped UMNO regain the Islamist "moral high ground" that the PAS had been claiming.

It was the beginning of America's global "war on terror" in 2001, however, that brought the political march of the Islamist parties to a screeching halt, as it provided an excuse for the government to crack down on the Malay right and the PAS.

But this only renewed UMNO's desire to portray itself as sufficiently Islamist. So, before stepping down, Mahathir went so far as to declare Malaysia a *de facto* Muslim state. Eyebrows were raised and questions were asked about the lengths to which Mahathir would go to counteract the Islamist appeal.

This trend continues. One of Badawi's first acts after taking over as prime minister in October 2003 was to introduce the concept of *Islam Hadhari*. This vague term was finally fleshed out with a list of ten principles in September 2004, all but one of which, however, was without religious connotations. Nevertheless, this move appeared to be all that was needed for Islam-minded voters to return to the fold of the ruling front.

In the general election in March 2004 – the first since Mahathir stepped down after 22 years in power – moderate Muslims helped Abdullah Badawi to a landslide victory. The release of Anwar Ibrahim soon afterwards raised the new premier's prestige further as a leader who could heal intra-Malay, and intra-Muslim, conflicts.

Since then, Abdullah Badawi has been popularizing the concept of "Hadhari," shaping it as a means to shift Islam's focus from its sanctioning function to its civilizing potential and rendering it less ideological. In Malaysia today, Islam is being presented as a generator of civilization and culture, and not merely as a source for religious inspiration. This has helped to counter extremist tendencies domestically and provides a conceptual platform for moderate Islam. Islam Hadhari tries to project the idea that UMNO's materialism and nationalism do not contradict Islam.

With various feints and strategies, Malaysia has effectively managed the tensions between a secular, modernizing agenda and the Islamic faith that the Malays profess. By making Islamists and Islamist sentiments a part of the process of modernization, Malaysia demonstrates that Islamic faith and economic growth can be reconciled if politicians are clever enough not to treat them as contradictions.

First published in *project-syndicate.org*, September 2005. Reproduced with the kind permission of Project Syndicate.

27

Taking Islam Hadhari global

THE WORLD cries out today for a description of Islam that distinguishes it clearly and essentially from expressions of political violence. More than that, such a presentation must also provide discursive space for socio-cultural change, democratic government and civil governance.

This is what Malaysia claims it has been trying to achieve. Not only is it one of the few countries with a Muslim majority that has a formidable record in economic growth, it has also managed to create a diverse professional Muslim middle class.

Although the real picture may not be as rosy as these words suggest, undeniable progress has been made by the government over the past few decades in improving the lot of the Muslim majority, and in the reconstruction - some may say the decolonisation - of the socio-political and ethno-economic structure of the country.

In the 1980s, partly as a response to rising Islamic consciousness among the Malays, inspired by events in the larger Muslim world such as the Opec oil crisis of 1973 and the Iranian Revolution of 1979, then prime minister Mahathir Mohamed decided to politicise Islam to generate support for himself and his party.

His recruitment of Islamist youth leader Anwar Ibrahim in the 1980s was part of this strategy. In the process, the Islamist Parti Islam SeMalaysia (PAS) gained stature as a bogeyman. Still, Tun Dr Mahathir's brand of politics transformed the country for more than two decades. His regime, despite much success in other areas, nevertheless left behind a Malay community divided along religio-political lines. The regime that succeeded him faced the difficult task of healing the fault lines.

Upon succeeding Tun Dr Mahathir, Datuk Seri Abdullah Badawi introduced the concept of Islam Hadhari. This was considered to be a strategic move made in preparation for the general election subsequently held in March 2005.

The ruling coalition, Barisan Nasional (BN), won a landslide victory in that election, securing control over all the 13 states of the federation barring Kelantan, the stronghold of PAS. PAS succeeded in retaining 24 seats there, three more than BN. Interestingly, the recent by-election in Kelantan's Pengkalan Pasir constituency has narrowed that small gap to one shaky seat.

With the release of Datuk Seri Anwar on Sept 2, 2005, the healing process that became the responsibility of the Abdullah regime continued. The major fault line now was not so much religious as it was moral, circling around the institutional corruption that the Premier had admitted existed and had promised to fight.

The depoliticising of Islam by the Abdullah regime now appears to have a role to play in the international arena. As present chairman of the Organisation of the Islamic Conference (OIC), Datuk Seri Abdullah has called for Muslim nations to form a common market.

Trade and education are the catchwords of his regime's offensive to revitalise Islamic culture. The OIC is presently holding its 3rd Extraordinary Islamic Summit in Mecca, at which it will discuss the recent report Islamic Ummah: New Vision, Solidarity in Action.

This was written by a group of Muslim scholars of various disciplines and, in it, it is stated that effective action was most needed in the field of education and in freedom of speech.

Here, the Malaysian experience may be able to make a distinctive contribution. Governance in the country has tried to balance itself between pure secular materialism and Islamic culture. This makes it interesting to a world searching desperately for a lessening of the tension between the West and Muslim states.

The idea hatched from Malaysian political conflicts was that a shift in focus was needed from seeing Islam merely as a source of spiritual guidance and religious comfort to being a inspiration for knowledge and wealth creation.

Even if Datuk Seri Abdullah's term – Islam Hadhari – is distasteful or offensive to some Muslim scholars and politicians, the idea for a discursive shift should not be brushed aside.

To sell this idea internationally, one fact has to be considered. Malaysia lies on the periphery of the Muslim world. This makes its voice less authoritative in the Muslim world. In order to be listened to, it must rely on its track record as an economically successful nation that has not denounced Islam in its system of government. But to put power behind its punch, it needs to anchor its initiative within the region. Since South-east Asia does have a larger number of Muslims than the whole of the Middle East, it would be advisable to develop a knowledge-craving Islamic discourse together with Indonesia.

Indonesia has surprised the world over the last two years with its successful transition towards becoming a functioning democracy. Furthermore, it is making dizzying success in solving the issue of Acehnese separation. How religion, especially Islam, situates itself within this new secular structure may yet inspire useful ideas about how the Islamic world as a whole can regain confidence in itself and maintain a healthy relationship with the non-Muslim world.

In these times of regionalism, when the Islamic world is searching for a common ground, when the East Asian region is taking radical confidence-building measures, and when the European Union is re-examining itself, Malaysia and Indonesia, perhaps with Brunei, have a chance to take the initiative and discuss the role of Islam in governance and in international relations.

If a South-east Asian Muslim position can first be constructed, at least at the governmental level, then the possibility for the region to revitalise inter-civilizational dialogue between the Muslim and the non-Muslim world would increase tremendously.

First published in Review, *Straits Times*, 9 December 2005. Reproduced with the kind permission of Singapore Press Holdings.

On Regionalism and Globalisation

28

Politics flounders in wake of nature's fury

THE TSUNAMIS that brought tragedy to coastlines throughout South Asia on Sunday left a trail of death and destruction that no terrorist venture short of a nuclear attack could have imagined. However, this disaster does provide us with the perspective that terrorists actually play god in a similar fashion - by bringing random death where death is least expected. Individuality plays no role, and nationality is irrelevant. Luck decides whether one lives or dies.

It was Boxing Day: A long weekend, the skies were blue and sunny, and there was no sign that any tragedy could be on the way. This was also the last weekend of the year, the time when we sigh with relief that the troubles of the old year can be overcome with the optimism and sense of purpose that the new year will bring.

The suddenness of the event, coming literally out of the blue, shocks us into admitting how vulnerable we really are. Just another adjustment of continental plates, and rings of waves were sent speeding in all directions across the Indian Ocean at jetliner speed. A few waves hit land and then disappeared. No moral agenda involved. The sea and the sky remained blue, and it continued to be Sunday. Rich tourists escaping the cold European winter drowned on Phuket's beaches as easily as poor villagers going about their daily business around Chennai did.

Seldom do we have natural disasters big enough to hit all sides of an ocean at one and the same time. When this happens, we can clearly perceive our vulnerability - indeed our puniness - as human beings.

Borders, class and race of the victims lose all significance, and are swept away for a little while. Offers of help are accordingly also without borders, class and race. Our differences now seem so unnecessary, and our ambitions and moral stands so lacking in humility.

On hearing that the devastation was worst in Aceh and Sri Lanka, one cannot but wonder if this disaster will cause the warring parties in both regions to put their differences aside and offer each other help. After a period of mutual mourning, perhaps the psychological map would change sufficiently for political solutions to become more possible.

The Acehnese and Tamil Tigers will be most in need of aid from the outside, and the bulk of it will come through channels controlled by the governments that have been their enemies. Given sufficient statesmanship - and generosity - on all sides, this state of affairs can be used to initiate a long-term softening of positions.

Now when cooperation is called for throughout South and South-east Asia, it would be wise for us to further learn that a willingness to cooperate throughout the region should be possible without any force being exerted on us by natural or man-made disasters, be it SARS, the avian flu, terrorism, the haze, or tsunamis.

Tsunamis are concentrated mainly in the Pacific and, to a lesser extent, in the Mediterranean and the Caribbean. That is the reason why no early warning system exists for the Indian Ocean, whose coastal surroundings had been spared this plague. Although the International Tsunami Warning Network was formed 40 years ago in 1965, after the Alaskan tsunamis generated by an earthquake measuring 9.2 on the Richter scale, countries such as India and Sri Lanka are understandably not members. Thailand is involved in this early warning system, but this does not include its western coast.

Since most other abnormal events affecting the region have tended to increase inter-state cooperation within Asean, we should not only expect Sunday's disaster to lead to more regional ties, but also capitalise on the added goodwill and commonality. The inability of Asean governments to stop the periodic haze that has affected the region should not be allowed to continue to exemplify regional political impotence.

More than 200,000 people perished on Sunday. The victims were scattered throughout half of maritime Asia, affecting at least 10 countries lying 2,000km apart, that makes it special. The big-picture perspective this affords us should be articulated and posted as a reminder that we are as ants busy by the side of a rippling pool, and that our conflicts are rather trivial.

Modern states are limiting things in many ways, and separate a person from his brother to a greater extent than they need to be separated.

Now when we are trying our best to remove borders for economic reasons, we should recall that we need one another in all sorts of other ways as well. Perhaps even Mother Nature is now convinced that regionalism and internationalism are the way to go.

First published in Review, *Straits Times*, 28 December 2004. Reproduced with the kind permission of Singapore Press Holdings.

29

Resolving differences
in disaster's wake

THE BEST memorial to the thousands of victims of the Indian Ocean tsunami disaster will be for the politics of the region to change for the better because of the widespread suffering and through the international relief work that is now needed.

The longer political considerations are kept out of the picture, the easier it will be for the flow of aid to reach the survivors. Governments have now to act more as administrators than as guardians of narrow interests and ethnic prejudices.

The mass media of all nations now have an important role to play in discouraging politicians from reaping personal and strategic gains from this huge catastrophe.

The United Nations, governments over the world, and all sorts of international organisations are now raising and allocating funds and sending people and supplies into the region to rescue survivors, limit starvation and stop the spread of tropical diseases. In light of this, travel restrictions should be eased dramatically, and local expertise should cooperate fully with the generous armies of international aid workers that are now on the way. Much needs to be done, and even if we manage to fend off the very real threat of starvation and disease, the process of mourning and rebuilding will take months.

Closeness between the different nations can grow out of this, since no human agency or enemy was involved in the disaster.

No blame game should be allowed to grow from this. No one caused the quake and no government can be reasonably held responsible for the fact that no tsunami-warning system for the Indian Ocean was in place. There had never been a need for one before. We must merely accept the fact that we cannot insure ourselves against all disasters.

Such is life. Sometimes, there is simply nothing we humans can do before the fact of a disaster. It is how we carry ourselves after the fact that decides the lasting consequences and that gives meaning to the suffering where none was to be found.

Governments can, however, rightly be blamed if they do not do their best to help the flow of aid and ensure indiscriminate distribution of supplies and medicine to the surviving victims. Pressure from the masses must be put on the governments that hesitate, because this is as much our business as theirs.

The higher the death toll rises, the greater the burden on the rest of us to learn from it and to benefit from it. The death of the thousands of Indonesians, Sri Lankans, Indians, Thais, Malaysians, Maldives Islanders, Myanmar people, Andaman Islanders, Somalians and tourists from all over the world will not have been in vain if a more peaceful Indian Ocean rim can result from the disaster, and if conflicts in the affected region, no matter how stubborn, can be pushed towards resolution.

The vulnerability of human life is now a painful and unwelcome insight for all involved. Buddhists, Muslims, Hindus and Christians have all been indiscriminately hit. The map has changed, not only on the ground, but also in our hearts.

This is a time of opportunity. Things have changed. This will be hard to recognise because it all happened so suddenly, and because we tend to think that politics is about principles and economics. But politics is just as much about emotions and how we deal with them. Right now, we are all mourning and, *inshallah* (God willing), we can make use of that to tear down walls and wash away barriers between us. For example, would any terrorist now dare to set off a bomb in the region; are not international tensions between Australia and South-east Asian nations now relaxed? If politicians can behave as statesmen would, then we can make the most out of this global disaster.

We may say that this is a temporary state of affairs, and things will return to how they were before Boxing Day, 2004. But that is how things always are. They return to their old state because we allow them to return to being the same. If we choose to recognise that things have changed, then we can change things. It is exactly this kind of horrendous event that can help us break karmic circles of hate.

The growing tension between Thailand and Malaysia over southern Thailand is now swept away by the destructive power of the tsunamis. Given the new scenario, Prime Minister Thaksin Shinawatra of Thailand can now rely for a while on goodwill from Thai citizens of all religions and even from the Malaysian government. With vision and statesmanship, it is not impossible for him to create an atmosphere for balanced negotiations with the Muslim separatists in the country's south.

Without doubt, the civil war between Buddhist Singalese and Hindu Tamils in Sri Lanka has a history that stretches back over centuries, as does Acehnese irredentism. To a large extent, old scores matter because we want them to matter. This merely leads to new scores that in turn also need to be remembered, ad infinitum. To paraphrase Mahatma Gandhi, an eye for an eye will indeed leave us all blind.

We must remain unwilling victims of nature, but surely we do not need to continue remaining victims of history.

First published in Review, *Straits Times*, 30 December 2004. Reproduced with the kind permission of Singapore Press Holdings.

30

A historic opportunity for Asean unity

THE CALL by Singapore Prime Minister Lee Hsien Loong on Thursday for Asean leaders to hold a crisis meeting as soon as possible is a welcome move.

The inclusion of representatives of non-Asean countries hit by the disaster is, of course, a given thing, as is the participation of major Asian and Australasian nations such as China, Japan, South Korea, Australia and New Zealand, as well as the United States, the United Nations, the World Bank and the World Health Organisation.

While it is always good to get as many actors on board as possible, this can happen only through a slowing down of the process. At present, speed is of the essence.

In practice, we can expect this concerted move by neighbouring countries to go ahead without being overly delayed by diplomatic considerations. Those who can move fast will lead the way, and latecomers will join when they get around to it.

Malaysia, Singapore, Thailand and Indonesia are supposedly the most prepared for such a meeting. These countries should, therefore, be able to lead the way from this end of the Indian Ocean at least, aided by international bodies that are already in the area.

The battered countries like India and Sri Lanka should welcome such a move.

THOUGH still new at his job, Mr Lee is a highly respected Prime Minister. Likewise, Malaysian Prime Minister Abdullah Ahmad Badawi enjoys broad support at home and abroad.

Newly elected Indonesian President Susilo Bambang Yudhoyono has not only won a strong democratic victory, but his position has also apparently been strengthened by the recent election of Vice-President Jusuf Kalla as the leader of Indonesia's most powerful party, Golkar.

These are men who are in the process of defining themselves as their respective country's paramount leaders.

They are full of new ideas, their world views are still full of possibilities, and they understand the importance of regionalism to the political economy of their nations.

Thai Premier Thaksin Shinawatra, who had not been looking forward to the general election due this year, will do well to seize the moment and try a soft approach to the growing problem in Thailand's south.

With Asean and other organisations working closely on relief and rebuilding in the wake of the catastrophe, there will be a lot of room for dialogue. Should he adopt a more regional and conciliatory attitude, his chances for re-election cannot but be strengthened. He has nothing to lose.

Asean has often been criticised for being passive in responding to the domestic conflicts of its member states.

No doubt, the insecurity of youth of both the institution and the individual countries provides excuses for that strategy. In the wake of the tsunami disaster, however, it should free itself from this culture of caution.

This is not a Sars or avian flu crisis, nor is it a forest-burning haze or a terrorist bombing. The magnitude of this crisis is quite beyond our individual comprehension, and the solutions need to be innovative and radical.

The human map has been redrawn, and given the sympathy now flowing in all directions, political situations can be created that will contribute to lasting peace and security for the whole Indian Ocean rim.

Now, when Asean nations come to one another's aid, the principle of non-intervention becomes somewhat anachronistic. They need one another too much for them to be overly courteous, and a hypersensitivity to the sensitivity of fellow members should not continue to define the grouping's behaviour forever.

It is, in fact, a sign of closeness if they dare give one another constructive advice, and if they can participate in one another's troubles.

International relief aid has been impressive so far. Calls have come from all quarters, including Singapore, that the UN should coordinate this gigantic effort.

However, funds from international bodies and extra-regional governments should not be allowed to come with strings attached.

In any case, the role that Asean countries must play together should remain central to how things develop in the region. The community needs to rise to the occasion, and must be seen to do so.

If relief work stops at providing the basics - food, water, shelter and clothes - then the victims in war-torn areas such as northern Sri Lanka and Aceh would have survived one disaster only to face another scourge, this time a protracted war.

The local governments, essentially Indonesia and Sri Lanka, if given sufficient economic push and diplomatic shove by neighbours, can enter into regional negotiations with their respective separatist movements.

Preferably, this should include separatists from southern Thailand as well.

Within this enlarged context, and with several determined but neutral parties sitting at the table, chances of the warring parties settling their differences would be historically high.

All parties have been hit badly by the tsunamis, and outstretched hands can receive willing responses. There is no better time to act the statesman than now.

It is not often that the region is gifted with a whole generation of new and young leaders. With help from their citizens, they can help usher in a new age of peace and prosperity.

First published in Review, *Straits Times*, 1 January 2005. Reproduced with the kind permission of Singapore Press Holdings.

31

It must be about helping people

THE FEROCIOUS tsunami of Dec 26, 2004, is gone, but the feelings of desolation, despair, fear and insecurity among its victims will last much longer. To the extent that they are ignored or mismanaged, the collective disappointment may seek political expression in ways the region and the world can do without.

For the present, most are concerned with starvation and disease. Lacking some of the basic necessities of life, they can but continue being at the mercy of others - first of nature, now of their fellow human beings. Should their governments fail in times such as these, then they lose legitimacy in their eyes and cannot count on their loyalty in the future.

When sudden despair turns into sustained disappointment, then alternatives can become interesting. Furthermore, in places such as Sri Lanka and Aceh, where civil wars have raged for decades, the sense of participation in the processes of nation building has been fragile in the first place, and sympathy for the central powers weak at best.

Genuine care from their governments, on the other hand, cannot but raise respect for the rulers. A large amount of political capital stands to be gained from a positive show of humaneness. This will be useful to the process of national reconciliation and reconstruction that is to come.

The difficult part lies in resisting one's partisan habits for the good of one's fellows. In this light, a firm presidential statement is helpful. So far, only President Chandrika Kumaratunga of Sri Lanka has clarified her principles. Leaders in Indonesia and Thailand have not been as forthcoming.

In Thailand, Prime Minister Thaksin Shinawatra has not linked the tsunami aid to other problems and issues in the south. A statement from his office attesting to the willingness of Bangkok to look into the needs of Muslim and non-Muslim residents in the area in conjunction with the disaster can hardly be a diplomatic blunder. It would, on the contrary, help transform the situation tremendously.

To be sure, as international aid increases in volume, the expectations of the victims will grow. While this is not the time to talk in dollars and cents, governments of the affected countries need to distribute compensation and aid by stating in clear terms how much each category of victim is entitled to receive in the coming weeks.

This will provide guidelines and ease the burden of officials and volunteer workers on the ground. Perhaps more importantly, this can prevent victims from entertaining unrealistic expectations and save them much disappointment.

In this regard, the Malaysian government has been very fast off the block in stating exactly which victim gets what. The formula for compensation has been kept simple. Of course, implementation is something else altogether, and needs to be closely monitored by the relevant ministries at federal and state levels.

The Malaysian government has also taken the laudable decision to open its airspace to relief efforts. The Sultan Salahuddin Abdul Aziz Shah Airport in Subang is now being used by the United Nations World Food Programme to supply Aceh with aid. Even the United States has been given permission to use the Langkawi International Airport for its relief efforts.

Singapore, affected only by a limited number of tsunami deaths, sets a strong and concrete example in offering the UN - which has since accepted - the use of its exemplary infrastructure, office space and a formidable range of modern communication facilities. This means that the city-state will serve as a coordination centre for disaster relief in the long months ahead. As a further sign of goodwill, it has relinquished all port charges for vessels carrying relief material to the areas hit by disaster.

All these actions bode well for the international summit of world leaders being held tomorrow in Jakarta. It is now up to the governments of the countries most affected to allow such neighbourly goodwill and resources to flow unhindered to the people they are meant for.

At the moment of writing, international aid totals a respectable US$2 billion (S$3.3 billion), with Japan being the most generous donor. When the immediate relieving of suffering has been achieved, other forms of aid will be required to steady the victims on their feet again, economically and otherwise. The more concerted and politically neutral the rebuilding programmes put in place, the less the sufferers will have to suffer, and the bigger the long-term gains for the countries involved, and for the region as a whole.

Co-authored with Phar Kim Beng. First published in Review, *Straits Times*, 5 January 2005. Reproduced with the kind permission of Singapore Press Holdings.

32

Chance for Asean countries to rally together

IT WILL be a while before the full extent of the damage wrought by the tsunamis of Dec 26 is known. But even as relief aid is being taken to the affected areas, thought should be given to the construction of a permanent mechanism to cope with future disasters in the region. Such a mechanism should be allotted a central position in the Asean structure.

The 2003 Bali Concord II declared that the realisation of an Asean Community would depend on the successful development of its three pillars, namely the Asean Security Community (ASC), Asean Economic Community (AEC) and Asean Socio-Cultural Community (ASCC).

Most would agree that of the three pillars on which a future Asean Community is to rest, credible achievements have been made in the development of the ASC and AEC.

However, the development of the ASC and AEC, and of the Asean Community as a whole, could be incomplete if the ASCC project fails to materialise. This is because regional social and cultural integration is also necessary to advance economic and security integration.

At the Vientiane summit last November, Asean leaders reiterated their desire to create a caring society and, officially, the plan of action for the ASCC aims at four areas: addressing poverty and equity, building a competitive human resource base and adequate systems of social protection, sound environmental governance and strengthening regional social cohesion.

How the ASCC is to be built is something that has bedevilled both scholars and policymakers. Community building includes, among other things, an evolving sense of solidarity and empathy with neighbours, especially in times of great tragedy. When the solidarity and empathy lead to assisting one's neighbours, then you have taken steps to promote a sense of community.

The Asean countries' responses to the tsunami tragedy thus can help to promote the sense of an Asean community. The tsunami disaster cuts across territorial boundaries, without regard to sovereignty of states.

Yet, in an age of globalisation in which there is rapid movement of information, money and even people across the globe, the capacity to relieve suffering caused by such calamities has lagged behind because of local administrative bottlenecks, bureaucratic red tape, poor infrastructure and concerns about sovereignty.

It is thus encouraging to note that Asean countries are assisting one another in concrete humanitarian terms in response to the human suffering and material losses caused by the tsunamis.

This can be seen in Singapore's cooperation with Indonesia in Sumatra and with Thailand in the vicinity of tourist resorts in the south. This cooperation is particularly significant on account of the considerable human resources, including military units, in Indonesia and Thailand.

In difficult situations, humanitarian and disaster relief operations are best led by military forces because they are the best organised and equipped for that kind of work. Likewise, Malaysia has also done its part in responding to the call for aid and assistance, particularly for Aceh.

Asean has in the past been discussing coordinated approaches to disaster relief. This catastrophe provides an opportunity to work this out in practice, including the smooth cooperation between military and civilian groups. Perhaps from it, contingency plans and a regional network located in the Asean Secretariat can be developed to deal with future natural disasters such as earthquakes and volcanic eruptions, as well as epidemics of infectious diseases. This will be a step towards the development of an Asean social community.

The enormity of the relief work now getting under way throughout the region, especially in India, Sri Lanka, Thailand and Indonesia, naturally calls for concerted Asean efforts in making certain that the rebuilding of lives and giving of aid will be effective and will lead to stable and lasting structures conducive to the attainment of Asean social goals.

Therefore, in the face of the tsunami tragedy, Asean must not only rise to the occasion, but must be seen to be doing so.

The crisis offers the organisation a chance to demonstrate that regional integration is not merely about economics and security, but that a more rounded development must entail strengthening bonds among the people of Asean. Learning from the experience of tsunamis, Asean member states must adopt a sense of common cause.

The creation of an appropriate mechanism centred at the Asean Secretariat in Jakarta will provide the organisation with concrete institutions that can handle regional humanitarian and disaster crises in the future.

With the right institutions in place, the secretariat will be capable of playing a central and cohesive role in managing assistance from governments and from civil society.

Co-authored with Lee Hock Guan. First published in Review, *Straits Times*, 7 January 2005. Reproduced with the kind permission of Singapore Press Holdings.

33

Strong KL-Singapore ties can boost Asean cohesion

THE HARVESTING season seems to have started for Malaysia and Singapore.

Relations between them have been improving since Datuk Seri Abdullah Badawi took over premiership of Malaysia in October 2003. He and then Singapore Prime Minister Goh Chok Tong had in their 20-minute meeting at the Asean-Japan Commemorative Summit - held in Tokyo in December 2003 - found they could get along well.

Already at that point, they saw the possibility for both parties to put new effort into clearing old quarrels. No doubt, they also realised that the luxury of acrimony was becoming too expensive. It was decided that the series of 'bilateral issues' that had become obstructive hurdles over the last few years should not continue to keep the neighbours from enjoying good and beneficial relations.

Throughout last year, the prime ministers of both countries and high-ranking ministers and officials, as well as top businessmen, made courtesy and business calls on each other, and progress was made in a variety of areas ranging from business ventures to educational projects to joint mass-media productions.

Seminars, conferences and fora on bilateral relations became the fad among researchers, academics and consultants.

The accommodating atmosphere that grew from the efforts of Datuk Seri Abdullah, Senior Minister Goh and Singapore's new PM Lee Hsien Loong is now generating dividends.

The idea that putting aside stubborn 'bilateral issues' would in fact make the rest more easily resolved is now proving to be sound. The first of the 'low-hanging fruits' is now ripe for plucking.

It was revealed on Thursday that the independent group of experts set up on the orders of the International Tribunal for the Law of the Sea, following Malaysia's surprise move to start arbitration proceedings against Singapore in September 2003, had actually managed to reach a final agreement.

This good news is an exemplary triumph for patient negotiations, and speaks volumes for the efficacy of dialogue over bickering.

Other outstanding issues that have plagued relations between the two countries include Singapore's military access to Malaysian airspace, the pricing of raw water supplies to Singapore, the future of Malaysia-owned railway land inside Singapore, and a proposal for a new bridge to replace the Causeway linking the two nations.

Optimism that these matters of contention will be successfully resolved is now rising. This is helped by the continuing economic integration between the two countries.

The Malaysian investment bank CIMB recently managed to buy Singapore's GK Goh Holdings' entire broking arm, gaining an inroad into markets in Singapore and Hong Kong. This continues a rush of investments between the two neighbours over the last year involving major investment players on both sides.

In fact, in July last year, Singapore's Temasek Holdings continued its engagement in Malaysia by going into partnership, through its Mapletree Capital Management, with CIMB itself. That partnership had created Malaysia's first private institutional real estate fund. CIMB's acquisition in Singapore further deepens the economic integration between the two states.

A more realistic take on these developments is that Asean integration is happening at too slow a pace. Therefore, for the material well being of both Malaysia and Singapore, and by extension also for Asean as an economic entity, these two countries are now moving ahead to speed up the grouping's regionalism.

There are signs that the two countries will be cooperating in different ways to help integrate Asean further, economically and otherwise.

For example, next week, a joint mission comprising representatives of 70 companies from Singapore and Malaysia will be visiting Indonesia to explore business possibilities there. Profitable tripartite partnerships are expected to grow from this initiative.

Bilateral relations between Malaysia and Singapore - two of the more developed countries in the association - hold great potential for the future of South-east Asia as a whole. The two in collaboration may be able to provide the impetus needed for Asean to achieve integration.

As things stand, even an integrated Asean is nothing to boast about in comparison to other regional bodies such as North American Free Trade Area or the European Union. Therefore, Asean+1 free trade agreements with China, Japan,

India and South Korea are seen as necessary tools in the region's economic survival.

The great danger here is that FTAs with large neighbours will favour various Asean members differently, and may actually pry Asean apart in practice. There is therefore all the more reason for more developed Asean states such as Malaysia and Singapore to constitute a strong cohesive base for regional integration.

The benefits of regionalism today extend beyond economics: Extremism of all sorts can best be controlled on a regional basis; diseases are spreading faster than ever and are best prevented from doing so through international efforts; fighting crimes such as piracy are increasingly dependent on cross-border cooperation; the growth of China and India - two unitary economic giants with enormous domestic markets - poses challenges to Asean's small member-states that in the long run are best met multilaterally; and the harder struggle for foreign direct investments is most easily won by the regional economy rather than the national economies each on its own.

Just as Malaysia now looks hopeful towards the creation of an East Asian Community by 2020 with the initiation of the East Asian Summit in Kuala Lumpur in December, Singapore is also preparing itself.

The two countries, so similar in so many aspects, can anchor the integration process by combining their expertise, and by pooling their resources. This would be a major, if not decisive, contribution to East Asian growth.

First published in Review, *Straits Times*, 15 January 2005. Reproduced with the kind permission of Singapore Press Holdings

34

Much at stake
at the East Asia Summit

THE EAST Asia Summit to be held in Kuala Lumpur this December is an event that holds much hope for the future of the region. The stable and increasing economic gains that most are aiming for will most probably also provide long-term political stability and aid integration on other fronts.

Therefore, while some Malaysians have proclaimed the summit as the long-awaited realisation of former prime minister Tun Dr Mahathir Mohamad's East Asia Economic Caucus (EAEC) under another name, many do not see how the summit will differ from the Asean Plus Three framework if Australia, New Zealand and India are not allowed to participate on a par with the Asean 10 and the three East Asian countries of China, Japan and South Korea. It is still unclear why the summit, as conceived by the Malaysian hosts today, should start by limiting itself.

The suspicion is that this stand is a leftover of the APEC-EAEC controversy 15 years ago, when India and China were still not the big players they are today, and before the 1997 Asian financial crisis changed the region's economic picture and damaged its self-confidence. If any ideology is to stimulate East Asian integration now, it must be something along the lines of Strength Through Diversity.

Singapore and Indonesia support the idea of Australia and New Zealand taking part in the summit, while Malaysia has repeatedly been against it. It may be difficult for Malaysia to play the gracious host while at the same time refusing to let in friends of honoured guests.

Indonesia, led by popular new President Susilo Bambang Yudhoyono, of whom much is expected, is obviously grateful for the generous Australian aid to natural disaster victims in Aceh and Nias. The impact and importance of this aid are undeniable evidence of the role Australia has in the region. According to the Asean way itself, there is no good reason to keep Canberra out of a hugely expanded congregation of interdependent economies.

The two countries are now planning a new security pact and an agreement on a range of development issues. Australian Prime Minister John Howard has also just approved Australia's largest ever aid contribution of about $1 billion to help rebuild Aceh over the next five years. The leaders of both countries are to head a joint commission to monitor how the money is spent, another sign of the continuity both seek in the improvement in ties.

This is indeed close cooperation in the making, a proper burial of the proverbial hatchet - 'a historic step in Indonesian-Australian relations', as President Yudhoyono put it. He stated further: 'It assumes that our countries are locked together not just by geography but by a common future. It is not enough for us just to be neighbours, we have to be strong partners.'

The question now is if Malaysia under Datuk Seri Abdullah Badawi can continue not to assume this. His visit this week to Australia, the first Malaysian visit at the prime ministerial level since 1984, lets on it cannot.

In the light of international economics, Malaysia has more to lose than win in keeping Australia and New Zealand outside the summit. In fact, given the improving relations between Indonesia and Australia, a race may have started to attract Australian goodwill and investments. Thailand and Singapore already have free trade agreements with Australia. Malaysia is eager, for economic reasons, to reach a similar milestone.

Two-way trade between Malaysia and Australia is at $13 billion, and Malaysia is Australia's 10th largest trading partner. But while Malaysian investments in Australia amount to about $8 billion, Australians invest only $650 million in Malaysia.

Malaysia is indeed plagued by a perception problem - as Datuk Seri Abdullah recently noted - and that has been hurting the country unnecessarily. At present, it could do with less self-inflicted problems.

Exclusion in politics tends to generate future conflicts - and perpetuate old ones - and the pulling of rank to keep countries out of the summit does not bode well for whatever regional body is in the making.

Tun Dr Mahathir's tussles with Australia and other nations are events from another era, and the new generation of leaders will do well not to continue battles not of their own making, and which came about under old circumstances.

Given the history of good ties between Malaysia and Australia and New Zealand, especially during the 1963-1966 confrontation between Malaysia and Indonesia, it is odd indeed that relations between these countries are as bad as they have become.

Perhaps it is on the matter of summit participation that Datuk Seri Abdullah is required to put forth a clear Malaysian stand and present his own view of the world.

What does all this say about the future of Asean? Has it grown as much as it can and will it now be overtaken by the summit and the flurry of bilateral frameworks? Will it regress into a club that has seen better days, which members revisit when they feel nostalgic?

If the summit is reasonably successful and if it should lead to major innovations for regional integration, Asean may in practice dissolve into 10 countries within a gigantic economic sphere comprising 13, 16 or perhaps more countries.

The announcement made recently that the 10 stock markets of its members would be integrated by 2010 does not only seem too late, it seems too optimistic. Asean integration has been a slow and clumsy process. This has led to bilateral initiatives being taken by individual nations to build ties with countries outside the region. While this does not easily translate into integration as such, no faster route has been available for individual Asean nations to take.

Tensions between individual members over issues such as southern Thailand or the ocean sectors in the Sulawesi Sea that Malaysia and Indonesia both lay claim to, or the bilateral issues between Singapore and Malaysia, given Asean's cautious way, do in fact put a freeze on regional integration at a time when delays can be fatal.

The impending problem of Myanmar taking over the chairmanship late next year seems to be one courtesy too many to demand of fellow members. While time may defuse some problems, others tend to grow with time.

Given this scenario therefore, the summit, being important to the status of the new generation of leaders in East Asia, may rewrite the process and pace of integration.

First published in Review, *Straits Times*, 9 April 2005. Reproduced with the kind permission of Singapore Press Holdings.

35

Myanmar question, Asean dilemma

THE ADMITTANCE of Myanmar into Asean in 1997 promised a rocky ride that has now materialised.

Asean then argued that the inclusion of Myanmar would allow its members more opportunities to nudge the military government towards reform. However, increased criticism of the Myanmar government by Asean states over the past year shows a waning of trust in that strategy.

Now with the reality of the Asean chair being situated in Yangon in the middle of next year looming larger, the range of voices attempting to convince the junta to forfeit its prize has grown, including those of Malaysian parliamentarians led by Datuk Zaid Ibrahim demanding that Myanmar be stripped of its Asean chair unless democratic reforms are carried out.

The reasons for the increasing pressure on Myanmar are quite clear. First, the junta has failed to release Nobel laureate Aung San Suu Kyi from house arrest.

Second, reforms are still wanting. The regime has obviously not felt any nudges that it has not been able to ignore. With Myanmar's military junta holding the Asean chair next year, some Asean members feel that the regional body is being made to suffer for its generosity and for its trust in the power of neighbourly goodwill. The demand is that Myanmar should now give something back.

Third, given the strong public feeling in Europe and the United States in support of Ms Suu Kyi, Brussels and Washington can in no way be convinced to participate in any meeting with Asean to be held in Yangon.

A more central issue involves the viability and sincerity of Asean's strategy of 'constructive engagement'. Myanmar refugees and asylum-seekers totalled 210,000 in 1997. Today, eight years after Myanmar joined Asean, they officially total half a million scattered throughout the region. The real figure is probably a hundred thousand higher.

The increased drug traffic and further suppression within the country are further signs that Asean affiliation in itself has not helped matters.

Are things coming to a head? The million-dollar question here is how profoundly Asean and the Asean way will be affected. There are two sides to view the situation from.

On the one hand, not much has changed. The argument that Asean would suffer international criticism if Myanmar chairs next year's summit is weakened by the fact that Asean accepted Myanmar in the face of international criticism. There is little reason to believe that these criticisms - ranging from the lack of human rights and freedom of speech to low levels of democracy - would disappear were Myanmar to agree to skip its turn.

There is also little chance that Myanmar, let alone Asean, should fear economic isolation should the junta stand firm, especially given the fact that it has supporters among Asean governments. Furthermore, Myanmar has strategic links with China and India, while Singapore continues to be its largest investor.

It is also a breach of capitalist logic to believe that American or European companies would pull out of South-east Asian countries just because Myanmar has the Asean chair. Cheaper labour, raw materials and government incentives will continue to be of primary concern for such companies, and not politics.

If Myanmar was authoritarian when it was a non-Asean member, on what concrete grounds was it assumed that the usurper junta would volunteer democratic reform and surrender centralised power on becoming an Asean member? One would have thought that once regional acceptance and legitimacy had been handed to it, it would even feel less need to reform.

What concrete grounds made Asean rely on 'constructive engagement'? Was it wishful thinking or were there decisive measures being planned? Instead of merely blaming the junta, we should perhaps question the sincerity of Asean members in proclaiming 'constructive engagement' as a cure-all strategy.

As a buzz term that hinted at a subtle Asean way, 'constructive engagement' has, in practice, meant backroom dialogue between national representatives away from the media. There are certainly merits to such a process. But while civil and discreet-sounding, constructive engagement has never guaranteed applied action, largely because formal mechanisms and structural obligations to ensure that member countries negotiate towards a desired outcome are lacking.

On the other hand, Asean and the East Asian region at large are changing at a breathtaking pace, and this may explain the increasing turnabout within Asean against

Myanmar's feet dragging. Too much is at stake for further courtesy to be paid to an ungrateful back-pedalling partner.

Malaysia, one of the main supporters of Myanmar's entry into Asean in 1997, will take over the chair later this year. While the position does not bring any official power, it does carry some influence and may provide possibilities to defuse the situation. Initiative for change with regard to Myanmar should perhaps continue to come from the Malaysians.

What Asean must do in the coming months is nothing less than the redemption of the idea of "constructive engagement". If concrete mechanisms and measures - economic or political - can be quickly constructed to facilitate wide-based Asean engagement in remedying conditions in individual member states which have strong bearing on Asean as a whole, then the chairmanship baton may yet be passed on next year without too much hesitancy.

Co-authored with Terence Chong. First published in Review, *Straits Times*, 16 April 2005. Reproduced with the kind permission of Singapore Press Holdings.

36

The world's just a circle in a spiral

ONE FRUITFUL way of understanding "globalisation" is to see it as a term necessitated by the fact that global influences are no longer unidirectional, that is, coming largely from the West.

No doubt the model of a bipolar world in which the Soviet Union and the United States fought wars by proxy lives on in certain quarters, and seeks re-enactment.

The dualistic tradition of understanding the world is too long and entrenched to suddenly disappear – good against evil, the faithful against the infidels, Jedi knights against imperial storm-troopers.

While one can see a general tendency to recreate a bipolar world in which a veritable replacement for the Soviet Union is sought - either in terrorism, Islam, the Axis of Evil or a rising China - it has become increasingly necessary to admit the growing multi-polarity of the post-Cold War world.

An adjusted view was presented in Samuel Huntington's influential essay Clash of Civilisations. Here the aggressive bipolarity of the Cold War is replaced by several poles - civilizational core states -arrayed against the West.

It caught the imagination of many for a while, and still excites some today.

Within the concept of globalisation, we are faced with a need to depict global dynamics in ways that will not lock us into old habits of thought, and that do not assume conflict and competition as the wherewithal of international relations.

Handling the phenomenon of a "rising China" is crucial to this task. One should not forget that the China that is economically growing is not communist China. In fact, it is to the extent that China has stopped acting like a communist regime that it has developed economically.

It is a non-communist China that is on the rise.

The fact that a leader of the Kuomintang now visits the mainland and is given the red-carpet treatment testifies to this. Communism is being understood by most as a pragmatic solution taken in a historical context, and that is now in turn being replaced by other pragmatic solutions.

Indeed, "rise" connotes threat only to those privileged by the status quo.

The economic might of China should therefore not be confused with the might of a militant communist regime obsessed with global ideological goals. The lifting of hundreds of millions above the poverty line in the past decade is to be applauded and should not be seen reflexively as a threat. China's influence will grow by default, independent of its political agenda.

What is happening at lightning speed today is that a network of trade ties and friendly diplomatic relations across East Asia is being constructed at a rate unthinkable not many years ago. Indeed, an optimist may understand the recent flare-up between Japan and China to be the start of the final confrontation needed - at least at government-to-government level - for the peaceful dissolution of tensions inherited from World War II. It may be just what is needed to enable the forging of mutually beneficial ties.

Momentous events are happening in Asia today. The Bandung commemoration in Jakarta last month was a milestone in that it saw a kind of meeting of the leaders of Asia and Africa that differed greatly from the first 1955 meeting, no ideology divided them.

There was no reason for dispute or aggression and cooperation seemed the only thing for them to discuss.

Recent developments in intra-Asia ties such as Chinese aid to Indonesia and to the Philippines, the Treaty of Friendship, Cooperation and Good-Neighbourly Relations between China and Pakistan, Chinese-India trade cooperation, India-Pakistan dialogues, Malaysia-Singapore solutions of bilateral issues, and free-trade agreements in all directions suggest a strong emerging pattern in contemporary globalisation.

Australian initiatives to build ties with Indonesia are part of what it deems to be a necessary adjustment to accommodate multidirectional forces - which include nature's disasters.

The upcoming East Asia Summit in December in Kuala Lumpur is significant in this context. It brings together the major players throughout East, Southeast and South Asia, and the synergy likely to emanate from this in the future is causing New Zealand and even Australia to reconsider the basis of their relations with South-east Asia.

This flow of events occurs alongside other networks of regional bodies formed and being formed throughout the world, and the inter-regional economic connections between these regions are also strong and robust.

Clashes between them, and clashes within them, are no longer rational.

Instead of a unipolar, bipolar or multipolar world, we may be seeing the coming into being of a *bola takraw* world.

Like that rattan ball popular in the Malay world, there are so many poles that the lines of linkage are more obvious than the points they join.

First published in Review, *Straits Times*, 2 May 2005. Reproduced with the kind permission of Singapore Press Holdings.

37

No mutualism, no regionalism

HISTORY STANDS in the way of closer East Asian ties, as many have noted.

The latest example was highlighted by Japanese Foreign Minister Taro Aso as he left for Kuala Lumpur on Dec 7 to attend a series of summits among East Asian countries. (These meetings will culminate in the first East Asia Summit EAS on Wednesday.)

Mr Taro told Asian leaders that they had to overcome the past through a spirit of reconciliation and collaboration - a praiseworthy call.

But it must also be understood that the process of not allowing history as such to limit future possibilities has a vital epistemological requirement - epistemology being the theory of knowledge, especially in terms of its methods, validity and scope.

What is required - and this is the contribution that historians today can make towards improving relations between East Asian states - is a multiplicity of descriptions about modern history that are as scientific as possible.

Honest studies of the major forces in the history of international relations will show that shifts in focus regarding these forces lead to shifts in our historical understanding - and subsequently shifts in moral blame.

Such an exercise, in a best-case scenario, will leave us with a humbler and more tentative attitude towards "historical knowledge' as such.

The European experience where regionalism is concerned has become a sort of benchmark. But we must realize that "Europe" was initially the project of conquerors and would-be conquerors.

In modern times, the continent has suffered the armies of Napoleon Bonaparte, which were followed 150 years later by the armies of Adolf Hitler. And Eastern Europe after World War II had to bear the brunt of Stalinist imperialism.

From this chaos of repeated war and imperialism spread the insight that a peaceful centralization of politics was necessary if further warfare was to be avoided among the many powerful countries on the continent.

In the breathing space created by the Allies' triumph, institutions of reconciliation and collaboration began to grow.

What made this process possible was the concept of mutuality. No decision could be forced onto any nation, no matter how correct it may appear to others. All potential partners had to be considered equal regardless of geographical or economic size.

'Mutualism' therefore is the key to peaceful co-existence, be it between states, nations or individuals. This idea is not new. We find it in the writings of wise men of all civilizations - from Confucius to Jesus, from the Prophet Mohamed to

Buddha, and from Mahatma Gandhi to Petr Kropotkin. But how central that idea is to peaceful human existence becomes most obvious only in a crisis, or when disaster threatens.

While the EAS takes place in an atmosphere of optimism, the bright future that participants seek to construct must nevertheless contend with the dark shadow of the past, or at least of the described past.

It does not bode well for East Asian regionalism that China and Korea have refused to meet Japanese Premier Junichiro Koizumi on the sidelines of the summit, the tension stemming directly from the received view of modern history.

Where the modern history of East Asia is concerned, we must remind ourselves that no concept about a united 'East Asia' with a status equal to that of a united 'Europe' had broadly existed until the idea of a Greater East Asian Co-Prosperity Sphere was announced as late as August 1940, and used as an excuse for empire-building by a militarized and modernized Japan hungry for resources.

The international atmosphere within which that came into being was one that had for over a century been configured by rampant European colonialism. Japan was thus part of this flow of forces, and was in a real sense reacting to save itself by becoming at least as ruthless as it understood its enemies to be.

The fall of European power in the Far East after World War I left Japan the major expansive power in the region.

No Asian government had appeared that could demand to be treated as Japan's military and economic equal, and so it marched on alone to create its own modern destiny, adopting the racism and the colonialism of the warring European nations in the process. This tore the fabric of Japanese society apart, and in 1930, militarists assassinated their moderate Prime Minister Osachi Hamaguchi.

The Japanese colonization of mainland Asia continued in 1931 with the invasion of Manchuria, and would soon stretch into Australian waters and to the Indian border. With the end of World War II, the forceful unification of East Asia by Japan also came to an end.

Napoleon's Empire failed, Hitler's Third Reich failed, and the Greater East Asian Economic Co-prosperity Sphere also failed.

What are succeeding instead are the European Union, and the budding East Asian Community (EAC), as both now continue to consolidate. The EAC still has a long way to go, no doubt, and its highest hurdle still remains 'history'.

China and Korea may be blamed for using the history card for chastising present-day Japanese actions, but at the same time, Japan remains fixated with the glory of its first stage of modernization. The modern history of East Asia had been about surviving and reacting to stronger outside forces. Japan, one could say, was the most reactive of them all, since it went the furthest and with the greatest speed in thoroughly dismantling its own socio-political system. Its success was, put crudely, a measure of the extent of its socio-cultural suicide.

A fresh look at historical forces in the first stage of East Asian modernization should recognize this reactiveness of Asian nation building and even of Japanese imperialism, and how this quality has affected domestic and world policies over the past 150 years.

Of course, one could argue that the EAS project itself is a reactive phenomenon as well. What makes this not quite true, however, is the fact that mutualism is involved, and it is the idea of inter-state equality that will make it something that Asians could be proud of.

China and Korea will find it easier to bury the pain of their modern past if Japan also buries both the shame and the glory of its modern past, and vice-versa. Once the modern period is epistemologically bracketed, mutual respect for each other's needs and shifting descriptions of history and identity will have a chance to grow.

A common view of being caught in the same inescapable and painful dynamics of modern internationalism may then emerge among East Asian peoples.

While one should not expect too much from the first EAS, the fact that Australia and New Zealand are included shows that the world is aligned differently today. Past analyses are losing relevance. The inclusion of India supports this conclusion, as does the fact that Russian President Vladimir Putin has been invited to speak to the EAS forum even though his country is present only as a guest.

Whether the EAS is truly East Asian or whether it is a new creature not easily labelled is not an essential issue. History moves on in the present, and so the past must tolerate review.

First published as "True mutualism the key to East Asian regionalism" in Review, *Straits Times*, 12 December 2005. Reproduced with the kind permission of Singapore Press Holdings.

38

Regionalism hinges on national stability

PROPONENTS OF regionalism have been celebrating their achievements in the East Asian region recently. However, a major question begs to be asked. Despite the rather limited ambitions of East Asian regionalism, will growing regionalism require more national cohesion within its member states, or less?

News about the serial successes of the first East Asia Summit (EAS) before, during and after Dec 14 - the day of the historic convention in Kuala Lumpur - was accompanied by reports about a coup attempt against Philippine President Gloria Arroyo, which was apparently aborted in its very early stages.

This sign of instability in the Philippines - one of the founding members of Asean, which is now positioned to lead the process of regionalism in East Asia - gains further significance from the fact that Mrs Arroyo will host the next EAS, at the tourist resort of Cebu. These summits are now to be an annual affair, to be held only within Asean despite China's offer to host the second meeting.

The Muslim rebellion in the southern islands of the Philippines is another long-standing challenge to Manila. Events there no longer warrant front-page coverage mainly because they have become a permanent fixture in Southeast Asian politics.

Thailand's Muslim south continues to spell trouble for Premier Thaksin Shinawatra, weakening his political position far beyond what he himself had thought possible after his second successive parliamentary electoral win early this year. Inter-ethnic killings in the south have continued and the potential for cross-border incidents involving Malaysia remains ever present.

The root causes of the violence in southern Thailand go back to at least the beginning of the 20th century. Indeed, inter-ethnic problems in the region have been around a long time, and Asean as a whole has lived with them for as long as we can remember. Where inter-ethnic relations are concerned, Singapore and Malaysia shine as relative gems despite underlying tensions here and there.

With increasing regionalism, these domestic conditions will no longer remain merely domestic concerns. Anything that might undermine national stability - or anything that might affect investor confidence in the region in general - will gain renewed salience and become a matter of regional concern. The high-flying ambitions associated with the EAS may lead to added pressure on the governments of member states to rethink the importance of national stability.

Myanmar is an apt example of how low state capacity disables a government from participation in regional bodies. The person of Aung San Suu Kyi has helped to gravitate world attention to the failings and lack of legitimacy of the present regime. Such external pressure caused Asean to wave - admittedly weakly - a warning finger at Myanmar's regime during the Asean Summit and the EAS.

As regionalism takes off, more focus will come to be put on the importance of state capacity, or at least national stability. The lack of state capacity among member nations - and not stubborn historical squabbles such as those between China, Japan and Korea - will be the weak link in the creation of an East Asian Community. International undertakings and agreements do not amount to much if signatories cannot guarantee their continuity. The minimal requirement of effective regionalism is the capacity of member states to deliver on their promises.

In this context, measures to fight corruption will draw much media attention, as has been the case in Malaysia since Datuk Seri Abdullah Ahmad Badawi took over as prime minister in October 2003. Given the high expectations, disappointment with his policies has been mounting despite his successes.

In Indonesia, comprehensive reforms under President Susilo Bambang Yudhoyono - whose greatest achievement so far arguably is the peace treaty with the Free Aceh Movement (GAM) - continue. His latest move came a week before the EAS, when he reshuffled his Cabinet in what many saw as an attempt to disrupt the personal business dealings that officials had with government bodies.

Another unstable national entity is Cambodia, where corruption is rife and the economy is dependent on foreign aid. While it is also an Asean problem child, Cambodia has not been an international headache for the organisation, for various reasons.

Vietnam continues with its transition from command economy to free market. Alongside that transition, it has carried out reforms in its administrative and legal infrastructure, as has been the case in neighbouring China.

These countries stand out as success stories in the transition from socialism to capitalism.

Outside of Asean, some EAS members also have problems with their governance, although they are generally very stable compared to some within Asean. Corruption, however, has been a perennial problem both in India and China. Their governments understand this.

On the weekend before the EAS, Australia – otherwise a symbol of stability in the newly conceived regional expanse – was shaken by racial rioting. Youths of North European appearance clashed with youths of Middle Eastern appearance over at least two days in suburbs of Sydney. Such disturbances, though significant, do not amount to national instability, at least not for a long time yet.

Though Asean is now directing the regionalisation process, it should be remembered that every one of the non-Asean members of the EAS enjoys a state capacity and a national stability far beyond those of many Asean members.

It is of crucial importance to remember that regionalism will not weaken the relevance of nation-states. Rather, there is a dialectical relationship between national stability on the one hand and international cohesion on the other. Regionalism requires national stability, and national stability is enhanced by regionalism.

First published in Review, *Straits Times*, 28 December 2005. Reproduced with the kind permission of Singapore Press Holdings.

39

Breaking down colonialism's walls

WHERE THE border is to go bothers many who are trying to understand what it is that is so fantastic about the infant East Asian Community (EAC).

The paradigm by which the EAC is being judged is essentially a mix of the nation state and of the European Union. But perhaps the telescope is being looked at through the wrong end.

The EAC is in truth not about creating an outside wall; it is about tearing down inside walls.

The mercantilism that gave the European Atlantic states the impetus to sail and steam far and wide in search of gold, spices and everything in between was accompanied by the wish to monopolize resources. Their competitors were other European nations. And so, the initial strategy of taking over trading ports and trading routes soon became one of conquest and of subjugating local polities.

The "founding" of Penang and Singapore was followed by the signing of the Pangkor Treaty that started British control over the Malay states.

Most importantly, the geopolitics in colonized regions was totally changed, and traditional ties built upon commercial interests were destroyed to be replaced by new ones forged in accordance with expediencies felt in faraway London, Paris and Amsterdam.

Therefore, the Dutch handed over Malacca to the British for safekeeping after Holland fell to Napoleon's armies.

After foiling the French attempt at building a European empire, the British and their Dutch allies drew a clear line in the distant Malacca Strait to demarcate their separate spheres of interests. Malacca was officially handed over to the British in exchange for Bencoolen.

Good fences make good neighbours, especially when both are occupying foreign turf and are not feeling totally welcomed by the locals.

And so, peoples living under the British came to know practically nothing about the world beyond the British perspective. Their commercial interests, their education and their concepts evolved with minimum input from other modern powers.

The same thing happened throughout the region, be it in territories under the Dutch, the French or the Spanish.

More tragic than that, the people-to-people contacts over colonial borders jealously guarded by the Europeans came to a virtual standstill. East Asia's geopolitical pre-colonial history was dismantled, and the newly formed colonial territories became strangers to each other.

This process provided the geopolitical structure for what would become the new and independent nations in Asia and Africa, each politically, culturally and commercially fenced off from each other.

The story is told often enough about how China was on the verge of being "cut up like a melon" by European powers and Japan in the beginning of the 20th century, and how the outbreak of World War I deflated these ambitions.

After the European powers had beaten each other bloody by 1918, Japan was left alone to imbibe the whole fruit. It appeared to Japan's militarists, and understandably so, that their glorious modernised state was fated to feast alone at the vacated colonial table in East Asia.

The rest is also history.

Unlike China, the dividing of the proverbial melon did take place in other territories, and on planes other than the purely political.

In South-east Asia, the Dutch took over the trade routes of the Bugis, managing in the end to command all the major islands of the archipelago except for the easternmost ones that the Spanish had earlier settled in.

The British took the Malay Peninsula, and in time gained influence over northern Borneo, while the latecomers, the French, had to settle for the coastal regions south of the Manchurian Empire.

Very latecomers, such as the Germans and the Belgians, were left with nothing in the South-east Asian region to colonise. Economically, politically, culturally and, very importantly, epistemologically, the South-east Asian melon was neatly sliced.

What needs to be recognised today, when colonialism is gone and regionalism has become the fad, is that we are not merely witnessing the founding of new structures. Very often, acknowledgement of certain undeniable dynamics of localism is being expressed as well.

Commercial and cultural forces are still defined to a great extent by geography, climate, population concentrations and other highly stable factors.

Once the politics in the region were no longer controlled by outside interests, the great rivers of East Asia, for example, began to dictate commercial ties and, along with them, political agreements. The Mekong basin today practically demands cooperation by the polities that share its banks.

The Changjiang, or Yangtze River, of China comes into its own, and the city at its mouth, Shanghai, grows beyond comprehension.

The shores of the Yellow Sea come alive as never before to reflect the economic might of the peoples of at least three littoral countries.

In line with this rationale, one should expect a sturdy economic revival of the silk routes in Inner Asia, as well as trade ties between China and Myanmar.

In South-east Asia, maritime forces are dictating ties more freely again. Economic and cultural interests now radiate in all directions. Traditional ties with India and the Arab world are growing again, as are customary links northwards with China. What are new here are bonds southwards, with the settler colonies of Australia and New Zealand.

No doubt, much of the dynamics affecting the region are new, but just as much are not. The idea of an East Asian Community needs therefore to be understood as part of a process of reconnection, of learning to know old neighbours anew, and of learning to know new ones. The fact that this occurs alongside the speedy global dynamics of the 21st century should not blind us to the fact that we are in many ways rediscovering pre-colonial ties and dismantling colonial walls even as we build post-colonial bonds.

At the same time, recognising pre-colonial conditions should not involve a denial of the colonial heritage as such. The nation states themselves and the corresponding identities are all part of that legacy, as are the widespread migration of peoples and the popular use of European languages. Hopefully, the long historical pluralism of East Asia and the pragmatic mindset will guarantee against any such tendency.

First published in Review, *Straits Times*, 17 January 2006. Reproduced with the kind permission of Singapore Press Holdings.

INDEX

www.ingramcontent.com/pod-product-compliance
Lightning Source LLC
Chambersburg PA
CBHW021541260326
41914CB00001B/104